Laboratory Manual

LAWRENCE
MCGAHEY

THE COLLEGE OF SCHOLASTICA

The Chemistry of Everything

KIMBERLEY WALDRON

PEARSON

Prentice
Hall

Upper Saddle River, NJ 07458

Editor-in-Chief, Science: Dan Kaveney
Senior Editor: Kent Porter Hamann
Assistant Editor: Jennifer Hart
Executive Managing Editor: Kathleen Schiaparelli
Senior Managing Editor: Nicole M. Jackson
Assistant Managing Editor: Karen Bosch Petrov
Production Editor: Ashley M. Booth
Supplement Cover Manager: Paul Gourhan
Supplement Cover Designer: Christopher Kossa
Manufacturing Buyer: Ilene Kahn
Manufacturing Manager: Alexis Heydt-Long

© 2007 Pearson Education, Inc.
Pearson Prentice Hall
Pearson Education, Inc.
Upper Saddle River, NJ 07458

Printed in the United States of America

10 9 8 7 6 5 4 3 2 1

ISBN 0-13-187536-1

Pearson Education Ltd., *London*
Pearson Education Australia Pty. Ltd., *Sydney*
Pearson Education Singapore, Pte. Ltd.
Pearson Education North Asia Ltd., *Hong Kong*
Pearson Education Canada, Inc., *Toronto*
Pearson Educación de Mexico, S.A. de C.V.
Pearson Education—Japan, *Tokyo*
Pearson Education Malaysia, Pte. Ltd.

Preface

When I began the task of preparing this lab manual, I felt a bit like a child with a paper bag full of Halloween treats who must choose which few pieces of candy he is allowed to eat today. The name of Kimberly Waldron's text, *The Chemistry of Everything*, rightly suggests that there is no limit to the possible number of topics that could be the subject of the experiments for this lab manual. Like the candy-rich kid, I was faced with the dilemma of "what to choose" for inclusion. For this first edition I have attempted to provide enough work to span a semester-length course using the entire text. Many of the experiments are variations on the "usual suspects" and some might be called "new," but all are written assuming that *The Chemistry of Everything* may be the student's first introduction to chemistry. Thus, each chapter was developed in the context of the information presented to that point in Waldron's text. To emphasize this the companion sections in Waldron are cited immediately at the beginning of the chapter.

The first two chapters cover basic safety items and a description of lab equipment. All others include an introductory section placing the topic in a broader context, followed by background material on the specific experiment. Relevant safety issues are set aside next in a block, followed by the procedure. Closing out each chapter are pre-lab exercises and a worksheet for recording data and answering post-lab questions.

My own experience has demonstrated repeatedly that the success of the exercise is related to the preparation a student invests before coming to lab. Thus, the pre-lab asks the student to write a short statement of objectives and prepare a list of the equipment needed—providing some "encouragement" to read the procedure before coming to lab. The other pre-lab exercises either review the chemical concepts underlying the lab or provide practice for the work to be done once the data have been collected.

Experimental procedures are written in a step-by-step "cookbook" fashion in consideration of the typical level of laboratory experience of a student enrolled in a liberal arts chemistry course. In contrast, I have earnestly attempted to construct the lab exercises so that a student must actually perform the work, collect data and ponder its meaning in order to answer a question or puzzle. In other words, my goal has been to make the labs active learning experiences rather than simple demonstrations of what could be known from reading the text only.

Most of the experiments can be completed within two hours, allowing students to finish the post-lab worksheet before leaving for the day, either individually or in a group. Doing so provides an opportunity to "strike while the iron is hot," for questions will surely arise. The teachable moments seem to come more often when students are concentrating on completing the assignment than after it is graded!

Very deliberately, I have omitted from the student text most information that would be needed only by the instructor or laboratory support personnel. The instructor's manual contains a complete list of the materials, chemicals, and relevant directions for preparing any solutions needed in each lab. Also included are comments and tips based on my own experience.

Although I have made every effort to ensure that the experiments succeed as written, I heartily encourage instructors to test procedures they have not previously used in their own classroom in order to make accommodation for any local differences in equipment, space, and safety regulations.

It is my sincere wish that instructors and students using this lab manual as a companion to *The Chemistry of Everything* will find it clear, readable, and educationally worthwhile. Looking ahead, I hope to expand the number and range of experiments in a later edition; a list of exercises that I did not get in publishable shape before the usual publication deadlines is on my desk even now. I welcome comments and questions on any aspect of this text in the hope of making it better the next time around!

To Students

I know many of you may be thinking, "chemistry is boring, incomprehensibly hard, and best avoided if at all possible." Since you are reading this, you evidently did not manage to avoid the subject! Having come this far, I believe that you will find the subject neither boring nor incomprehensibly hard after taking a course using Professor Waldron's text, *The Chemistry of Everything*. I hope the exercises in this lab manual help you reach that conclusion as well.

Doing lab work is much like any other new activity—it may seem awkward at first, but with preparation, patience, and practice it becomes much easier. The most important preparation you can make each week is to read over the assigned sections in the Waldron text and this manual before coming to lab. Your instructor most likely will assign some of the Pre-Lab Exercises to complete as well. If you conscientiously carry out these simple suggestions, you are much more likely to get your lab work done safely, correctly, and faster.

Please know that all the experiments in this text are designed to be safe and use the least hazardous materials possible. Your preparation, patience, and alertness to what you are doing are also essential to working safely. Although the procedures are written in a step-by-step fashion, you still must be actively thinking about what you are doing. And when you aren't sure about something, please ask! The lab instructor needs to feel useful, too.

As the course progresses, you will gain practice and confidence in your lab skills, and the whole chemistry business will begin to seem much less alien to you. By the time the course ends, perhaps you might even want to take another chemistry class….well, it's just a thought. Enjoy the ride.

Acknowledgements

No author gets a book into print by his own efforts. I am deeply indebted to the assistance and patient forbearance of Carol Snyder, Crissy Dudonis, and Colleen Morris. Bless you!

Lawrence McGahey
The College of St. Scholastica
Duluth, Minnesota
July 10, 2006
Email: lmcgahey@css.edu

Table of Contents

Chapter	Title	Page
1	Safety First	1
2	The Tools of the Trade	6
3	A Penny for Your Hypothesis	11
4	A Density Dilemma	17
5	A Separation Puzzle	25
6	All Charged Up—Ionic Compounds in Solution	31
7	Of Alkenes and Vegetables—Thin Layer Chromatography	39
8	Making Models, Making Connections	49
9	Back and Forth—Reversible Reactions and Equilibrium	57
10	pH Pointers—Acid-Base Indicators	63
11	Pop Goes the Acid—Estimating the Acid Content of a Soft Drink	73
12	Some Light Work—An Introduction to Spectroscopy	83
13	How Much Heat Does It Hold?—Measuring the Heat Capacity of Metals	97
14	A Trip to the Distillery—Separating Liquids by Distillation	107
15	Undoing Mountain Dew™ —Extraction of Caffeine	119
16	How Cold Can It Get?	129
17	It's a Gas—Synthesis of Nitrogen	137
18	Soap's Up in Fat City—Saponification of Lard	147
19	Milk Gotcha—Protein, Carbohydrate, and Minerals in Milk	157
20	Pain Relief through Chemistry—Synthesis of Acetaminophen	169

Like most of the public, you probably have seen or heard the phrase "toxic hazardous chemical" in news reports. Not surprisingly, you may think that a chemistry lab is a very dangerous place and wonder "why should I be here?" After all, the lab must be full of "toxic hazardous chemicals." Truthfully, a chemistry lab is a *potentially* dangerous place, but so are many household laundry rooms, kitchens, and garages.

Your reaction to the words "sodium hypochlorite," "lye," and "petroleum distillates" is probably quite different from how you respond to the words "bleach," "oven cleaner," and "gasoline." Yet bleach is a solution of sodium hypochlorite, oven cleaners often contain lye, and gasoline is but one type of petroleum distillate. We very often perceive the hazards of a material in terms of our familiarity with the substance, when in fact we need to consider the properties of the substance and how we plan to use it in assessing the harm it may cause.

If you are apprehensive at all about working in a chemistry lab, please be assured that your instructor's first concern is for your welfare. The experiments in this manual are designed to use the least dangerous materials and techniques possible. Every exercise will alert you to potential hazards and provide instructions to avoid creating unsafe situations.

On the other hand, you should not have a completely relaxed and inattentive attitude when you are in lab. It is a lot like driving an automobile—you need to be aware of your surroundings and be on the look-out for potential accidents. No experiment is successful or worth doing at the cost of injury to the person doing the work!

Over the course of time chemists have developed some basic guidelines or rules designed to make lab work as safe as possible. Some rules may seem common sense, while others are less obvious. Please realize that simply following the rules and experimental procedures like a mindless robot will not guarantee your personal safety— you have to think about what you are doing. *Your brain is your most important piece of safety equipment!*

In any experiment the nature of each chemical substance, how they react with each other, and the techniques being used will determine the particular safety procedures that need to be followed. As we mentioned above, these special instructions will be emphasized in each lab exercise. Equally important are the basic safety guidelines that apply to almost all lab situations. When you consciously follow the basic safety rules, you are creating an attitude and safe environment in which you can do your lab work. Please remember, working safely is no accident!

The chart on the following page lists some basic lab safety rules. Your instructor may provide additional ones to comply with local laws and regulations in your area.

Some Basic Lab Safety Rules

1. Familiarize yourself with the lab procedure *before* coming to class.

2. Wear long pants, shoes with socks, and a lab apron or coat.

3. Wear eye protection when you or those near you are working with chemicals, glassware, or equipment. Goggles or safety glasses should have a shield that blocks materials from entering the eyes at the side of your head.

4. Keep your fingers out of your eyes, ears, nose, and mouth when you are working with chemicals. Wash your hands frequently. If the chemicals used are caustic or prone to causing stains, wear gloves.

5. Do not eat or drink in the lab, and be sure to wash your hands after leaving lab before eating.

6. Learn the location of emergency exits and safety equipment such as the eye-wash fountain, safety shower, and fire extinguishers. Know how to use the equipment before an emergency occurs.

7. Perform only approved and supervised experiments.

8. Replace broken or cracked glassware. Do not heat cracked glass.

9. Use a suction bulb to draw liquids up into a pipette. Do not draw liquids into tubes by mouth suction.

10. Keep flames (matches, lighters, burners, and alcohol lamps) away from open containers of flammable materials.

11. Use highly volatile or smelly substances in a fume hood.

12. Label containers of chemicals while you work so the contents can be identified quickly.

13. If you spill a chemical, immediately ask the instructor for assistance in cleaning it up properly.

14. Dispose of chemical waste in the designated containers provided by the instructor.

15. Do not remove chemicals from the laboratory.

16. Be alert to what others around you are doing – anticipate unsafe combinations of activities.

Pre-Lab Exercise
Offer a brief rationale or explanation for each of the basic safety rules given on the previous page.

Safety Rule	Reason for the Rule
1	
2	
3	
4	
5	
6	
7	
8	
9	
10	
11	
12	
13	
14	
15	
16	

Name: _____   **Lab Section:** _____

In-Class Safety Exercise

The purpose of this activity is to help familiarize you with the safety equipment and procedures in your school. You may want to keep the completed activity in the lab manual for reference.

1. How many door exits lead from your lab classroom?

2. Where is the nearest eye-wash fountain?

3. How is the eye-wash fountain operated?

4. What are the two nearest exits from the building housing your chemistry lab?

5. In case of a fire alarm during lab, where are you supposed to assemble outside the building?

6. Why is it not safe to use an elevator during emergency evacuation of the building?

7. What is the proper attire for lab when chemical experiments are being performed?

8. Who must be informed if there is an accident or chemical spill during lab?

9. Where is the nearest emergency phone? What is the telephone number for campus emergencies?

10. Where is the safety shower and what is it used for?

11. Where is the nearest fire extinguisher? What must be done to make the extinguisher operational?

12. Make a sketch of your lab classroom that shows the location of the following items in their actual relationship to each other:
    a) lab benches
    b) door exits to the hallway
    c) doors to adjacent rooms
    d) eye-wash fountain(s)
    e) fire extinguisher(s)
    f) safety shower(s)
    g) fume hoods
    h) container for broken glass
    i) nearest exit from building
    j) nearest fire alarm

2 | The Tools of the Trade

Every profession or trade has specialized equipment and tools to make its tasks easier. For example, carpenters have numerous kinds of saws, plumbers have different types of wrenches, and cooks have a wide array of pans and bowls. Not surprisingly, chemists have quite a selection of apparatus for experimental work.

So consider what chemists do: They measure, mix, react, separate, and study stuff. Since matter (stuff) is anything that has mass and takes up space, devices are needed for weighing and measuring volume—and the tools may need to be different for solids, liquids, and gases. Implements to pick up and transfer chemicals are desirable to avoid contact with the skin (and sometimes atmospheric moisture and gases). To perform reactions chemists need the equivalent of pans and bowls, as well as devices for stirring, heating, and cooling. When it comes to separating mixtures chemists use filters, sieves, funnels, and yet more esoteric equipment. The properties of matter can be studied not only by observing chemical reactions, but also through examining physical properties such as melting and boiling temperatures, density, and so on.

In this section we will briefly introduce some of the more common equipment that you likely will use in carrying out the experiments in this lab manual. When specialized equipment is needed for an experiment, it will be described in the material for that exercise.

Containers are usually made of clear, heat-resistant glass (commonly called Pyrex®). Glass is convenient because it is generally chemically un-reactive, can be molded into many shapes and sizes, and gives a clear view of the contents. Containers that will not be heated directly are also sometimes made of translucent plastic for safety.

Beakers are shaped like coffee mugs, but without handles. The wide open mouth makes it easy to add materials to the beaker and evaporate liquids easily.
Beakers come in many sizes; some have graduations marked on the glass to indicate the approximate volume of the contents.

Erlenmeyer flasks are general purpose containers like beakers, but the upper walls slope inward to create a narrow opening. This shape makes it easier to hold the flask and mix the contents by swirling. When liquids are heated in an Erlenmeyer flask, evaporation is slowed down because vapors tend to collect and drip back into the liquid. Erlenmeyers also come in many sizes and may be graduated.

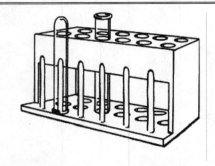

Test tubes are cylinders of glass closed off at one end with a hemispherical bottom. The size of a test tube is given as inside diameter (in mm) x length (mm). A common size for a small tube is 10– x 75–mm (approximately ½ x 3 inches).
Two are shown here in a rack that safely holds filled tubes upright (back), or upside-down for drying (front).

 A wash bottle is usually made of polyethylene and contains water, but other liquids can be dispensed this way. Read the bottle label—don't assume the liquid is H_2O!

Liquid is forced up a tube and out the nozzle when the bottle is squeezed. Take care not to point the spray nozzle in the direction of your own face or a fellow lab worker when picking up or using the wash bottle.

Volumetric Glassware is manufactured to indicate the volume of material—usually a liquid—held in the container. Chemists often dispense a particular volume of a liquid chemical instead of measuring it out by mass. (But of course, a liquid can still be weighed!)

A *graduated cylinder* is just that: a tube sealed at one end having a scale along its length marked in volume units, usually milliliters (mL). The diameter of the cylinder is narrow compared to the length so that small differences in the height of the liquid are more easily discerned. A pouring lip at the top facilitates dispensing without liquid running down the outside of the cylinder.

A *graduated pipette* is a long, thin tube open at the top and constricted to a small outlet at the bottom. The volume scale is marked along its length. It is held in one hand. Liquid is drawn up into the pipette by suction with a rubber bulb. The desired volume of liquid is transferred by slowly releasing the suction.

Small, unmeasured volumes of liquids are transferred with a *medicine dropper* or Pasteur pipette and a small suction bulb.

A *burette* is comparable to a graduated pipette. However, the burette is larger, held upright by clamps attached to a ring stand, and has a valve at the bottom to control drainage. The type of burette used in most labs holds about 50 mL of liquid and is graduated in tenths of a mL. (The top part of the graphic concerns how to read the scale; this will be covered in a later chapter.)

Transfer tools are used to move chemicals from one container to another and minimize your direct skin contact with chemicals. Not surprisingly, different pieces of equipment are needed for solids, liquids, and gases. Solids are handled with scoopulas or spatulas. Liquids are transferred by graduated cylinders, pipettes, and medicine droppers as describe above.

A *scoopula* is made from a curved piece of metal, and as its name suggests, is used to "scoop up" a sample of solid. The point on the edge is useful in breaking up big chunks of material in a bottle.

A *spatula* serves a similar purpose for a smaller quantity of material and has a flat metal surface.

Heating is routinely employed in the lab to speed up reactions or help materials dissolve in liquid mixtures. Chemists use gas burners, electric hot plates, mantles, ovens, and steam baths. (Microwaves are also beginning to find their use in the lab!) The type of heat source used is governed by what is being heated, what temperature is needed, and how precisely the temperature must be controlled.

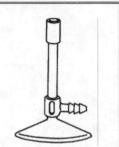

The *Bunsen burner* is a commonly recognized piece of lab equipment.
Most important, do not heat flammable materials in an open container with flames!

To light a burner: (1) turn on the gas valve (stopcock) at the bench; (2) cautiously bring a lighted match or striker to the top edge of the burner; (3) adjust the gas flow and air intake to provide the desired size flame. The flame should not leap above the bottom of the container being heated.

When it is not safe to use an open flame, a steam bath or electric hot plate is a good choice. A *steam bath* is a copper or steel pan with a cover made of removable nested rings. Live steam is admitted into the bath through a hose connected to an inlet pipe on the side of the pan. As the steam condenses (becomes liquid water), the heat released is transferred to a beaker or flask sitting on the cover. The waste hot water is drained through an outlet hose to the sink. A steam bath can not heat anything above the boiling point of water.

Electric hot plates work much like an electric stove: an electric current passed through a high resistance conductor heats it up. The conductor is generally shielded by a flat ceramic surface on which beakers and flasks can rest to be heated. An adjustable knob on the heater controls both the voltage and how hot the plate gets. Warning: The plate stays hot even after the electric power is shut off!

Hardware of various types is needed to assemble experimental apparatus or hold very hot objects.

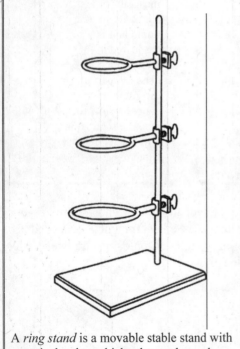

A *ring stand* is a movable stable stand with a vertical rod to which other tools can be clamped. Here, iron rings are shown. When heating a beaker or flask over a gas flame, a wire mesh is placed over the ring with the burner centered about 1–2 inches below.

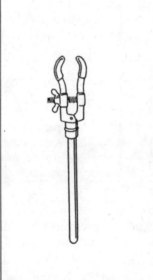

A *utility clamp* is attached to the rod of a ring stand with a clamp holder similar to the grip on the iron rings at left. Turning the wing nut against the spring adjusts the clamp to hold objects of different diameter.

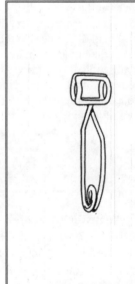

A *test tube holder* lets you safely grasp and move hot tubes.

Filtration is an important technique for separating solids from liquids.

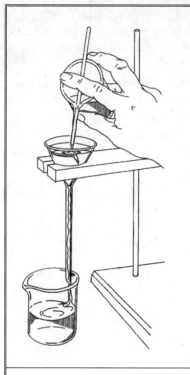

A *funnel* by itself is a valuable tool for transferring liquids without spillage, especially into containers with small openings. The funnel can be supported by a wooden rack clamped to the ring stand or an iron ring.

When the funnel and filter paper are used with a beaker or flask, the combination is called a *gravity filtration*. A mixture of liquid and solid poured into the filter paper is separated as liquid drains by gravity into the flask. A glass rod directs the flow of the liquid into the funnel. The last traces of mixtures can be "chased" out from the container with liquid from a wash bottle.

Filter paper is manufactured to be porous enough to pass liquids easily but retain solids. The paper is folded into a cone or fan to be placed inside a funnel as shown here:

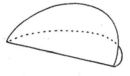 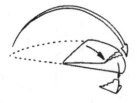

Thermometers monitor the temperature of gases, liquids, and solids. Traditionally, thermometers have been filled with mercury because this liquid metal conducts heat rapidly and significantly changes volume as its temperature changes. The reservoir or supply of mercury contained in the bulb at the bottom of the thermometer is immersed in the object whose temperature is being taken. The interior of the thermometer is simply a long narrow tube, or capillary, of constant diameter. As the volume of the mercury changes the length of the liquid column varies. The scale is calibrated so that 0° C is the freezing point of water is and 100° C is the temperature at which water boils.

Because thermometers break easily when dropped or mishandled, mercury spills can be common in labs. Now that we know more about the health hazards of mercury, newer lab thermometers are often filled with relatively non-toxic organic liquids colored with a red, green, or blue dye. The bulb is still fragile, and yes, you can get cut by breaking glass, so always handle thermometers with care.

Closing Note

Most likely, your lab locker has other equipment in addition to what we have surveyed in this chapter. If a piece of glassware is chipped or cracked, or any device looks defective, check with your instructor before attempting to use it in your lab work. It is also a very good habit to clean your equipment before putting it back in the locker at the end of the lab period—you will really appreciate this the next time you come to lab and need to use the apparatus!

Many of the experiments in this lab manual will introduce tips and techniques for using your equipment. Some of the techniques will seem obvious and easy, while others need to be learned and require a little practice. Whenever you are unsure what the instructions in a procedure mean, check with your instructor. Very often, a simple demonstration or explanation will clear things up.

all art work copyright and courtesy of Pearson Custom Publishing

3   A Penny for Your Hypothesis

Companion Sections in Waldron: Chapters 1.5 and 1.6

Introduction

Science is a process for learning about the natural world using the tools of observation, hypothesis formation, and testing. (Inspiration and intuition also have their roles, too.) Among other things, *observation* includes witnessing natural phenomena, making measurements, and keeping records. It might seem easy to make observations and measurements in a cold and detached way, but scientists need to be aware of their own preconceptions and biases because these can color what and how an observation is made.

A *hypothesis* is a tentative proposal or explanation for a set of observations. We all make observations in our daily lives and often come up with possible explanations for what we have witnessed. These explanations are hypotheses. A scientific hypothesis can be shown to be untrue by *testing*. This means an experiment or scenario can be created or an example found that disproves the logic of the hypothesis. For example, if my observations lead me to hypothesize that automobiles can be started only by inserting a key in the steering column, my hypothesis can be proved false by witnessing someone use a "remote" starter or seeing a thief "hotwire" the car! A key is not essential to starting a car. Hypotheses most certainly can be shown to be wrong, but they can never be proven true or correct. If many experiments over a long time do not disprove a hypothesis, we gain more confidence about its validity, but the hypothesis still is not proven correct.

One set of observations, hypotheses, and testing very often leads to another, creating a cycle of discovery that brings more information to light or makes connections with other facts and ideas that were not originally evident. Thus science is done.

The balance is one of the oldest tools for making observations. Ancient Egyptian and Roman artwork includes images of a double pan balance used to compare the weights of objects. The development of trade and chemistry both owe a lot to the humble scale. In this experiment you are going to examine the ordinary penny—lots of them in fact—by observing its weight on a balance. Since you already have everyday experience with coins, you have some working hypotheses about pennies, though you may not realize it. After scrutinizing the collected data (observed weights) you can test some of your hypotheses and reject them, keep them, or form some new ones to be tested. In short, this is a simple exercise to help you become more formally accustomed to "doing science."

Background on Balances

Scientists use the word *mass* to describe the quantity of matter in a sample. In contrast, *weight* refers to the force of gravity tugging a sample of matter towards the center of Earth. Two objects that have the same mass will also have the same weight when they are weighed in the same location on Earth. However, while mass never changes, weight does: an astronaut on the launch pad at Cape Canaveral has the same mass on the moon. But because the force of gravity is different on the moon and earth, the astronaut's weight on the moon is much less than in Florida.

Old-fashioned pan balances work by comparing the weight of a sample to a known reference mass; in effect, when gravity exerts as much tug on the sample as on the reference mass, the sample has the same mass as the reference. Modern electronic balances work on a similar principle, though it may be much less obvious. When an object is placed on the pan of a direct-reading electronic balance, a pin is pushed into a sensor, generating an electrical signal proportional to the force of gravity acting on the object. The electronic circuit in the balance compares the electrical signal with a stored reference value and displays this in units of grams. So while you personally do not place a comparison weight on the balance pan each time, the calibration or comparison indeed was performed.

Modern balances include a very nice feature called the "tare" button that subtracts out the weight of a container or object already placed on the pan. The display then shows only the weight of the next object added to the pan.

All balances, ancient as well as modern, are affected by air currents which cause the balance pan to "bounce" up and down, resulting in fluctuating weight readings. Usually the balance pan is surrounded by a barrier or windscreen to minimize this effect.

Before attempting the experiment, please make sure that you know how to properly use the specific model of balance in your lab. Once you have started making weight measurements you should not move the balance from its spot on the bench or jostle it.

Background on Pennies

This experiment is designed to use U.S. one-cent coins minted in 1970 or later. Coins for circulation are minted in Denver and Philadelphia. Coins imprinted with a "D" beneath the date were minted in Denver, while those without a letter were minted in Philadelphia.

If you are working alone or with a partner to collect and analyze data, you will need at least 15–20 pennies minted from 1970–present. You certainly can use different coins minted in the same year, but all the coins should not be from a limited number of years. Do not use coins on which you cannot read the date, have cuts in the metal, or appear to be encrusted with extraneous materials. Your fingers should be dry and clean before transferring the coins to the balance, or you may pick them up with forceps.

Procedure

You can do this experiment working alone but it is easier to work with a partner.
Your instructor may have you analyze your own data or use the combined observations of everyone in the class.

1. Check that the balance pan is clean and dry. Turn the balance on and set the display to zero (usually, you just need to push the "tare" button).

2. Place a clean piece of paper or a plastic weighing boat on the balance pan and tare the scale.

3. Choose one penny from your supply. Write down its mint date and location letter in the Data Table on the Worksheet.

4. Place the penny on the weighing paper or in the weighing boat on the balance pan.

5. When the balance displays a constant weight enter this value in the Data Table next to the corresponding date. [If the balance reading fluctuates, it typically varies in the last decimal place. Record the value that seems to occur most commonly as the weight.]

6. Remove the coin from the balance and set it aside separately from those pennies not yet weighed.

7. Choose the next coin, tare the balance, and repeat steps 3–7 until all your coins have been weighed and the data recorded.

8. Use your data recorded on the Worksheet (and any data shared with other students) to complete the analysis.

Pre-Lab Exercise A

Describe the purpose of the experiment in a few complete sentences of your own phrasing.

Pre-Lab Exercise B

Scientists sometimes formulate hypotheses *before* making formal observations by considering what is already known about the subject they plan to study. Clearly, you already have knowledge of U.S. coins, and some additional information has been provided in the reading above. Based on the information and experience you already have, list several hypotheses that you can form about the mass of pennies that might relate to the year they were minted, where they were minted, their age, and so on. It should be possible to refute or prove the hypothesis wrong on the basis of the year and weight data you will collect in lab. Two examples are listed to give you some help.

H1:   All pennies have the same mass.

H2:   Only pennies made in the same year at the same mint have the same mass.

H3: _____

H4: _____

H5: _____

H6: _____

H7: _____

H8: _____

H9: _____

H10: _____

Pre-Lab Exercise C

Scientists carefully consider how data are collected; they need to know if the observations are skewed, defective, or biased because of the method used to gather the information. In planning experiments and evaluating the work of others, scientists always need to ask if the way data were obtained determines the measurements. Observations that are flawed give unreliable data, and the hypotheses and conclusions based upon the data must be considered suspect.

With these thoughts in mind, consider the following questions about the procedure you will use in this experiment.

1. Sometimes foreign currency circulates alongside U.S. coinage. Suppose that you inadvertently weighed a Canadian penny in this experiment. What effect could that have on the validity of your data?

2. Why would it be best to weigh all the pennies on the same balance?

3. Suppose that you were concerned about combining weight data obtained using different balances. What simple experiment could be done to check that the data from different balances were the same?

4. The instructions recommend that you do not use coins that have cuts in them. Why?

Lab Worksheet Name: _____ Section: _____

1. Use the Table below to record the mint date and weight of each penny you used in the experiment.

Coin #	Mint Date & Letter	Weight in grams		Coin #	Mint Date & Letter	Weight in grams
1				11		
2				12		
3				13		
4				14		
5				15		
6				16		
7				17		
8				18		
9				19		
10				20		

2. Look back at the hypotheses you proposed before obtaining the data recorded above. List each hypothesis *disproved* by your results, and briefly explain why it was refuted.

3. Scientists are always interested in looking for patterns in the data they have collected. Patterns can suggest that a predictable phenomenon underlies the observations, or just as important, patterns can suggest if there are consistent errors being made in the course of collecting the data.

Look back at your table of data. Is there evidence of any pattern in the data you collected?   What is it?

A Penny for Your Hypothesis

Sometimes patterns become more obvious when data are arranged in different ways. Suppose that you list your weight data in chronological order, that is by the mint date. Use the new table below to present the weights listed in order of decreasing age of the pennies.

Weight data listed by age from oldest penny → newest penny

Coin #	Mint Date & Letter	Weight in grams		Coin #	Mint Date & Letter	Weight in grams
1				11		
2				12		
3				13		
4				14		
5				15		
6				16		
7				17		
8				18		
9				19		
10				20		

Now is there any pattern evident? Explain.

4. In answering question 2, you have already seen that experimental data may allow some hypotheses to be rejected. It is also common to have new questions and hypotheses arise as a result of collecting and analyzing the data. What new questions or hypotheses can you pose as a result of question 3?

5. The cycle of scientific discovery begins again when we propose additional experiments to discern plausible answers to questions or test hypotheses that come about as the result of earlier experiments, observations, and analysis. Looking back at your response to question 4, describe one or more experiments you could perform to test these hypotheses or attempt to answer your questions. You may not actually be able to conduct these experiments, but being able to imagine what *could* be done is the important point.

Introduction

By now you know that "matter is anything which has mass and takes up space (has volume)." Mass and volume are fundamental physical properties of matter, but they are not intrinsically connected. A pound of feathers and a pound of lead both weigh a pound. But a pound of feathers takes up a lot more space because the feather particles are not tightly packed together like atoms of lead. *Density is the quantity of mass per unit volume*. In other words, density equals the mass of an object divided by its volume.

Substances can be pure or mixtures. For example, a sample of tin contains only tin atoms, and a sample of copper contains only copper atoms. Mixtures in turn can be heterogeneous or homogeneous. Heterogeneous mixtures have definite boundaries between the components and are often easy to separate. A beaker filled with slugs of tin and copper shot jumbled together is decidedly heterogeneous—you can easily discern the round, orange-brown copper pellets from the flat pieces of grey-white tin—and you can sort the two metals into separate piles.

On the other hand, bronze is a homogeneous mixture of tin and copper melted together. Any size piece of the sample of bronze will have the same proportion of the two metals mixed together. The color and properties of this mixture are distinctly different from those of pure copper or pure tin, which is why it was given its own name. You most definitely can not see the individual atoms of copper and tin nor pick them apart in a sample of bronze.

In this experiment you are going to investigate this question: Can the density of a mixture gives us information about the mixture's composition? You will attempt to answer this question by examining the density of pure copper, pure aluminum, and mixtures of both. The metals will be in the form of small balls or lumps.

Background

The definition of density above suggests a simple method for determining this property of a substance: find its mass by weighing, determine its volume, do the arithmetic. Using a balance does not seem to present any great problem, but finding the volume may not be simple—is the substance a solid, liquid, or gas? Liquids and gases are fluids, meaning they have no definite shape of their own. A gas will expand to fill all the available volume, so its volume is simply the volume of the container. On the other hand, unless the entire container is filled with liquid, the container has to have a scale or set of markings to measure the liquid's volume. Solids possess a definite shape and do not require a container. If the solid has a regular shape like a cube, sphere, or cylinder, there are formulas to calculate volume based on the solid's dimensions. However, many solids are irregular in shape or there may be no formula to calculate the volume. Since most of the elements are solid, we do need to have a technique for this scenario.

Archimedes (the ancient Greek scientist of the "eureka!" story) demonstrated that an object which sinks in water displaces a volume of water equal to its own volume. Thus, all we need to do is carefully measure the volume of some water before and after adding an insoluble, heavy object to the water. Ah, but the devil is in the details.

A Density Dilemma

A graduated cylinder is the most practical tool for measuring the volume of an insoluble solid. The cylinder is much taller than it is narrow so that small changes in volume are more easily noticed. You may be surprised to see that the surface of the water in a cylinder is not level, and this is most obvious when the diameter of the glass is small. Intermolecular forces of attraction between H_2O and glass cause the liquid to "creep" or "climb" part way up the wall of the container. (This phenomenon is called capillary attraction.) There is a noticeable dip or low point, called the *meniscus*, in the liquid surface. In the sketch at right the meniscus is pointed out by the arrow.

In any type of glassware that is marked with a scale the volume is measured consistently at the meniscus. Your eye should be at the same level as the meniscus, because if the scale is viewed from above or below the light will be bent at an angle as it passes through the liquid, and your volume measurement will be wrong as a result.

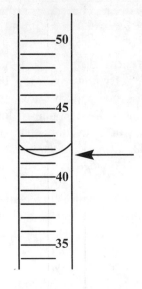

Figure 4-1

Figure 4-1 shows an expanded view of a partially filled 50-mL graduated cylinder. Notice that each line or subdivision represents a 1-mL change in volume. The meniscus falls between two of these divisions, so the volume is greater than 41 mL and less than 42 mL. The lab worker has to estimate the distance of the meniscus between the subdivisions. The meniscus is slightly more than half-way between lines, so the volume might be reported by one lab worker as 42.6 mL. Another lab worker reading the same scale (or the same person taking a second look) might decide the reading is at 42.7 mL. What would you report as the volume? Hint: imagine dividing the space between the two lines into 10 smaller subdivisions, so that each imaginary line marked off 0.1 mL.)

The scale has clear markings at the 42- and 43-mL levels, so these digits are "known," while the last, estimated digit is "uncertain." Scientists say the measurement 42.7 mL has *three significant figures*—the first two are known and the last one is uncertain. When scientists record data, the number of significant figures reported indicates how precisely or certainly the measurement was made.

Yet another problem arises when trying to measure volumes with a graduated cylinder or burette: Water sometimes clings to spots on the container walls and fails to drain into the main body of liquid. If the water later runs down the glass wall (of course not when you are looking!) the volume you have recorded will be incorrect, and since the volumes in your experiment are small, a few drops can cause a large error. Fortunately, this problem is easy to fix; the glassware just needs to be cleaned with soap and water and rinsed, until water completely drains off the glass without leaving spots.

And last of all, the water you use throughout the experiment needs to be at the same temperature because liquids expand and contract with temperature, changing their volume. Consequently, the density of the liquid changes with temperature.

To summarize, you can find the density of a piece of metal by weighing it, adding the metal to a measured volume of water in a graduated cylinder, and reading the volume level after the metal has been added. The difference between the volume readings gives the volume of the metal sample. Finally, dividing the mass (in grams) by the volume (in mL) computes a number for the density in units of grams per milliliter, or g/mL.

Procedure

1. Obtain a 25-mL graduated cylinder; note whether yours has 1-mL or 0.5-mL subdivisions on the scale. Using a test tube brush, wash it out with soapy water, and rinse it several times with distilled or deionized water. Check that water droplets do not stick to the walls of the cylinder, but drain downward easily. If not, try cleaning the cylinder again with soapy water.

2. Fill a wash bottle with 100–250 mL room-temperature distilled or deionized water.

3. Weigh out a piece of dry aluminum (Al) metal (3–4 g) on paper or in a plastic weighing tray. Record the mass of the metal in the Data Table on the Worksheet. [If your digital balance reads to two decimal places (0.01 g), the last digit on the display may fluctuate; this is your last significant figure in the mass. Decide which value for the fluctuating digit is most frequent and record it for the number in the hundredths place.]

4. Approximately half-fill the graduated cylinder with water from the wash bottle (12–13 mL). Tap the cylinder so that water drains off the walls. Record the exact volume in the data table on the Worksheet. Make the reading at the bottom of the meniscus, and check that you are holding the cylinder at eye level.

5. Tilt the graduated cylinder slightly on its side and gently slide the metal in so water is not splashed out of the cylinder. Hold the graduate upright, and tap it to settle any water drops and dislodge any air bubbles. (Bubbles can make the volume appear larger than it actually is.) Read the water level at the meniscus to three significant figures: the two known markings on the scale and your estimate of the first uncertain digit. Record this volume in the Data Table.

6. Clamp an iron ring or funnel support onto a ring stand. Rest a funnel in the support and fit it with a cone of filter paper. Place a beaker under the funnel, and pour the water and aluminum from the graduated cylinder into the funnel. Set the aluminum aside on tissue paper to dry, and discard the water. Return the funnel and filter paper to the ring stand.

7. Weigh out some dry copper (Cu) shot or strips (5–6 g) on paper or in a plastic weighing boat. Record the actual mass of the metal in the Data Table on the Worksheet.

8. Repeat steps 4, 5, and 6 with the Cu.

9. Prepare Mixture A consisting of about 6 g Cu and 2 g Al, taking care to record the actual masses used in the Data Table. Repeat steps 4, 5, and 6 with Mixture A.

10. Prepare Mixture B containing about 4 g of Cu and 4 g of Al. Again, record the actual masses used and follow through on steps 4, 5, and 6.

11. Prepare Mixture C from about 2 g of Cu and 6 g of Al. Record the masses and measure the volume of displaced water as before.

12. If time permits, you may want to make several other mixtures of Cu and Al. Keep the total mass of each mixture equal to about 8 g.

13. Separate the pieces of Cu and Al into two piles on paper to dry. The metal can be used again, so do not discard it.

A Density Dilemma

Pre-Lab Exercise A
Describe the purpose of the experiment in a few complete sentences of your own phrasing.

Pre-Lab Exercise B
Make a list of the chemicals and equipment you need for this experiment.

Pre-Lab Exercise C
Imagine that you were using a graduated cylinder with subdivisions marked off as in Figures 4-2a,b.

a) What change is volume is represented by the sub-divisions on the scale shown for this graduated cylinder?

b) What is the volume of the water shown in the graduated cylinder in Figure 4-2a?

In Figure 4-2b?

c) Suppose that a brass fishing sinker weighing 10.89 g was added to the partially filled cylinder in Figure 4-2a and the water level changed to what is shown in Figure 4-2b. What is the density of the brass sinker?
Show how you arrived at your answer.

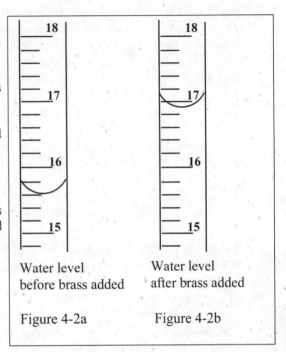

Water level
before brass added

Water level
after brass added

Figure 4-2a

Figure 4-2b

Pre-Lab Exercise D
1)   Explain how you can find the volume of an object if you know its mass and density.

2)   A fishing sinker made of steel weighs 28.1 g. The density of the steel is 5.8 g/mL. How much water does the sinker displace? In other words, what is the volume of the sinker?   Show your work.

Pre-Lab Exercise E
1)   Explain how you can find the mass of an object if you know its volume and density.

2)   Ethylene glycol is the principal component of anti-freeze for automobile radiators, and its density is 1.11 g/mL.   Suppose a service mechanic adds 0.75 L ethylene glycol to your car's radiator. What mass of ethylene glycol was used? [Hint: how many mL are equal to 1 Liter?]   Show your work.

Lab Worksheet   Name: _____   Section: _____

1. Fill in the Data Table below with your measurements from the experiment.

Sample	Mass of Al used (g)	Mass of Cu used (g)	H₂O volume before metal added (mL)	H₂O volume after metal added (mL)
Pure Al		0		
Pure Cu	0			
Mixture A				
Mixture B				
Mixture C				
Mixture D				
Mixture E				

2. Use your data from above to complete the Results Table below.
   Reminder: % Al in sample = (mass Al in sample ÷ total sample mass) x 100%

Sample	Total mass of sample (g)	Volume of sample (mL)	Density of sample (g/mL)	% Al by weight in sample
Pure Al				
Pure Cu				
Mixture A				
Mixture B				
Mixture C				
Mixture D				
Mixture E				

3. As you look at the Results Table in question 2, do you see any patterns? If so, what are they?

A Density Dilemma

4. Patterns in data are often more easily seen when the information is presented graphically. Use the scale given on the next page to present the following information from your Results Table:

a) On the horizontal axis, use the major divisions (each at 1-cm interval) to indicate the %Al in the sample. The range is 0% Al (= 100% Cu) → 100% Al (= 0% Cu).

b) On the vertical axis indicate the density of the sample. Arrange the scale so that your calculated density values are spread out as much as possible over the available vertical space.

c) Use a ruler or another straightedge to draw a straight line that comes closest to passing through all the data points.

d) Now what pattern is suggested by the graph? Write a complete sentence that briefly summarizes how the density of a Cu and Al mixture is related to the percentage or proportion of Al in the mixture.

5. Suppose that you had a mixture known to contain only Al and Cu fused together so that you could not manually separate the metals. Based on the results of this experiment, how could you estimate the composition of the sample?

6. Now think back to Lab 3 ("A Penny for Your Hypothesis"). Suppose that at some time the composition of metals used to mint the one-cent coins changed from being mostly copper to being a slice of zinc coated by copper. How might this explain the observations you made in Lab 3? How could you use the technique developed in this experiment to test your hypothesis?

Companion Section in Waldron: Chapter 1.3

Introduction

If you ask the average person what chemists do the answer will probably be something like this: "Oh, they mix stuff together and heat it to make other chemicals." It may surprise you to learn that chemists actually spend a great deal of time trying to un-mix (or separate) stuff!

Chemists are interested in the properties and uses of substances; a substance may be a single compound or a mixture, and usually substances are found in nature mixed together. For example, humans discovered a long time ago that making a tea from the bark of the willow tree was useful in treating pain and fever. Unfortunately, the tea was horribly bitter and caused stomach irritation. Eventually chemists isolated the pharmacologically active compound in the bitter brew and learned how to manipulate its structure to retain the pain-relieving action and reduce stomach irritation. The result is what we now call aspirin.

Even when chemists are mixing things together to concoct a new compound, the result is rarely a single pure substance. The desired product has to be "fished out" of the mixture of left-over un-reacted chemicals, other undesired materials that formed during the reaction, and the solvents in which the reaction occurred. Just as different types of bait and tackle are needed to catch fish of various sorts, chemists have assorted separation techniques. No matter what technique is used, the strategy comes down to exploiting chemical or physical properties of the desired compound and other substances in the mixture to tease the mess apart.

Chemical properties refer to the types of reactions that are specific to the compound you want to isolate from a mixture. For example, acids will react with bases, but non-acidic (or "neutral") compounds will not react. *Physical properties* include things relating to the physical condition of the substance, such as whether it is a solid, liquid, or gas; what liquids dissolve the material; its density; the temperature at which the liquid material boils; and so on. In short, any property of a substance can be used to isolate it from a mixture. The question becomes "which technique isolates the stuff I want as fast, easy, and thoroughly as needed?" Consequently, there is no one trick or technique that successfully separates all compounds, no more than a worm, a hook, and some string will help you land a marlin! Very often, both experience and experimentation are required to find the "best" way to isolate or purify a substance.

In this experiment you will need to devise a procedure to carry out the separation of a mixture containing three materials based on how they dissolve in water. You already know from everyday experience most of the information you need to solve the puzzle. For example, some things dissolve in water and some things do not; when you make coffee by the drip method, you rely on the fact that coffee grounds do not dissolve in water, but caffeine and the other flavorful elements of coffee do dissolve. You also take advantage of the technique of filtering with paper to keep the grounds out of your cup of java.

Tea drinkers are probably aware that it is easier to dissolve sugar in a small cup of hot tea than a large glass of iced tea; the temperature of a liquid affects how much and how fast something can be dissolved. And, you count on the lemon rind not dissolving in the tea!

A Separation Puzzle

Background

Food—"organic" or processed—contains chemicals that our bodies must metabolize to maintain life or process in order to be excreted. For example, one of the simplest building blocks for proteins is a compound known as glycine, which has the structural formula H_2N-CH_2-CO_2H. (For the present, do not overly concern yourself with the meaning of the formula or structure if you have not yet covered this in lecture because your ability to understand and complete the experiment does not require this knowledge.) Sodium benzoate, $C_6H_5CO_2Na$, is a chemical commonly added to foods to retard the growth of mold. Both in the body and in the lab (though under different conditions), glycine and sodium benzoate can react to make the excretory product hippuric acid, C_6H_5-CO-NH-CO_2H.

When hippuric acid is made in the lab some sodium benzoate and glycine remain behind. If you had synthesized hippuric acid so you had enough of a supply to study its chemical and biological properties, the left-over glycine and sodium benzoate would need to be removed before you could begin the investigation.

In this experiment you will examine how well and under what conditions a sample of each of these three compounds dissolves in water. Based on these results you will devise and test a procedure to obtain a pure sample of hippuric acid from a mixture of glycine, sodium benzoate, and hippuric acid.

Working Safely

A little warning bell probably sounded off in the back of your mind when you saw the word *acid* in the name "hippuric acid." That is entirely appropriate; however, the word acid simply means that the compound releases H^+ ions in water. In fact, glycine is also an acid. Sodium benzoate is a base, which means it scarfs up H^+ ions in water. As long as you do not handle the compounds with your bare fingers (and thus transfer some of the chemicals to your eyes, ears, nose, throat, etc.) they will cause you no harm. Your instructor may offer you disposable gloves to wear during the experiment.

You must wear eye protection while doing the experiment, both to keep you from placing your fingers in your eyes and also to prevent the water solutions from splashing in your eyes. If the water solutions are spilled on your skin, simply wash them off right away with soap and water. If you manage to get some of these compounds or the solutions in your eyes, flush them out at the eyewash fountain immediately.

At the end of the experiment, please dispose of your solutions and any solids in the waste container provided by your instructor.

Procedure

1. Label a 15- x 150-mm test tube "G" (for glycine).

2. Place a piece of paper or weighing boat on the pan of the lab balance and "tare" it.

3. Measure out about 0.1 g of glycine with a spatula onto the paper. Record the actual mass in the Data Table on the Worksheet.

4. Add 1 to 2 mL of distilled or deionized water to test tube G. Record the volume of water in the Data Table on the Worksheet.

Reminders

Tare means to set the balance reading to zero.

—

Keep the powder off your skin!

5a. Hold test tube G in one hand and gently tap it with a finger on your other hand to agitate the mixture for about a minute to determine if the solid dissolves or not. Record your observation in Data Table 1.

5b. Do this step only if the solid did not dissolve at room temperature in step 5a: warm test tube G in a beaker of boiling water on a hotplate for about 2 minutes. Does the glycine now dissolve?

—

Use a test tube holder to avoid being burned.

6. Now immerse tube G in a container of ice for 5–7 minutes. Does the glycine remain dissolved in cold water? Record your observation in Data Table 1. Set tube G aside in the test tube rack.

—

Avoid skin contact with the powder.

7. Label another 15- x 150-mm test tube "SB" (for sodium benzoate).

—

Record your data.

8. Repeat steps 2–6 using 0.1 g of sodium benzoate.

9. Label a third 15- x 150-mm test tube "HA" (for hippuric acid).

—

Keep the powder off your skin!

10. Repeat steps 2–6 using 0.1 g hippuric acid.

—

Record your data now.

11. If the solid hippuric acid did not dissolve even after heating, add another 2 mL of deionized water to test tube HA. Reheat the mixture. Does the solid dissolve now?

12. Remove tube HA from the hot water bath and let it cool briefly at room temperature before placing it in the ice. What happens?

13. Now the real experiment begins! Your instructor is going to give you a sample mixture that contains about 0.1 g of hippuric acid and less than 0.1 g each of glycine and sodium benzoate. Use the data you have collected in steps 1–12 to design a procedure that meets the following objectives:
a) Pure solid hippuric acid is to be recovered from the mixture .
b) Leftover glycine and sodium benzoate are to be recovered, but can be left mixed together. The equipment available includes all the equipment you used earlier in this lab, a funnel and filter paper.

In the space provided on the Worksheet, outline the specific steps you need to follow to accomplish objectives 13a and 13b.

14. Take your proposed procedure to the lab instructor for review and to obtain the mixture you need to separate. You definitely will have to attain objective 13a, but your instructor may not have you perform the work needed to fulfill objective 13b.

15. Measure and record the total mass of your mixture provided in Data Table 2.

16. Record the approximate total volume of water you used to dissolve the mixture.

17. After you have collected the hippuric acid, let it dry on some filter paper for about 10 minutes. Then determine its mass and record it. Also notice and record the physical appearance of the hippuric acid.

18. If your instructor asks you to recover the glycine and sodium benzoate mixture, also let   this dry before weighing it.

19. Follow your instructor's directions for safe disposal of the solids and solutions which remain after you complete the experiment.

Pre-Lab Exercise A
Describe the purpose of the experiment in a few complete sentences of your own phrasing.

Pre-Lab Exercise B
Make a list of the chemicals and equipment you need for this experiment.

Pre-Lab Exercise C
Based on your everyday experience and prior knowledge of science, briefly describe a simple way to separate the materials in each of the following mixtures as easily as possible. Explain in a complete sentence what property or properties of the materials are being used to make the separation.

1) a bucket of sand and pebbles (too many to sort out by hand!)

2) a bowl filled with nails made from either pure iron or pure aluminum

3) a beaker containing two kinds of plastic chips—one lighter than water and one heavier than water

4) a cup containing a mixture of table salt and sand

5) a pot of broth that has too much fat in it for your low-fat diet

Pre-Lab Exercise D
Suppose you go into the lab or kitchen and determine that you can dissolve at most 15 g of table salt in 50 mL of room-temperature tap water. By means of a simple proportion or ratio, how many grams of salt do you estimate could dissolve in 1 mL water?
Note: Chemists describe the *solubility* of a substance as the maximum amount of the compound that will dissolve in 1 mL of liquid in units of g/mL.

Lab Worksheet   **Name:** _____   **Section:** _____

1. Complete Data Table 1 below with your observations in steps 1–12.

Compound	Glycine (G)	Sodium Benzoate (SB)	Hippuric Acid (HA)
Mass used (g)			
Volume of water used at room temperature (mL)			
Did compound dissolve at room temperature?			
Was heat needed to dissolve compound?			
Was extra water needed to dissolve compound? If yes, what volume? (mL)			
Did compound remain dissolved when solution was cooled?			

2. Outline your proposed method for recovering the hippuric acid from a mixture containing about 0.1 g of hippuric acid and less than 0.1 g each of glycine and sodium benzoate. Your procedure should be designed to meet the objectives listed in procedure steps 13a and 13b.

3. Record your information and observations collected during the separation of your mixture in Data Table 2 below.   .

Total mass of mixture (g)	
Volume of water needed to dissolve mixture (mL)	
Dry mass of hippuric acid (HA) recovered (g)	
Dry mass of glycine + sodium benzoate recovered (g) *[if instructor assigns this step]*	

4. Describe the physical appearance of the hippuric acid before and after the separation process you used.

5. Write several complete sentences that explain *why* you are able to separate a mixture of hippuric acid (HA), sodium benzoate (SB), and glycine (G) by your method in order to obtain only hippuric acid (HA). That is, what physical properties of the chemicals did you exploit in order to obtain a pure sample of hippuric acid?

6. Assuming that you recovered all the hippuric acid (HA) in the mixture uncontaminated by glycine (G) and sodium benzoate (SB), what was the percentage by weight of hippuric acid in the mixture? Recall that the % by weight of a substance in a mixture is the mass of the substance divided by the total mass of the mixture multiplied by 100.

7. Chemists call the slow growth of crystals from a solution "crystallization." Briefly explain in a complete sentence or two how the term "crystallization" applies to the process that occurred in this experiment.

8. Use the observations you made in Data Table 1 to calculate an estimate for the solubility of hippuric acid (HA) and sodium benzoate (SB) in water at room temperature. [See Pre-Lab Exercise D.]

9. Why must the solubility of sodium benzoate (SB) and glycine (G) in cool water be greater than the solubility of hippuric acid (HA) for your separation to succeed?

All Charged Up
- Ionic Compounds in Solution -

Companion Sections in Waldron: Chapters 1.2, 2.2, 4.2, 4.3, and 5.7

Introduction

Compounds are substances made from atoms of more than one element. Chemists describe the two fundamental ways in which atoms combine to make compounds as *ionic bonding* and *covalent bonding*. (A later lab will examine covalent bonding.) Ions are substances that carry a net + or – charge because the total number of electrons and protons in the substance are not equal. The protons are found only in the nucleus of an atom (along with any neutrons) and do not participate in chemical reactions. On the other hand, the more loosely held electrons outside the nucleus of an atom can be transferred from one atom to another.

When an atom—which has an equal number of protons and electrons—gives up an electron, the ion formed has an overall positive charge because it now has more protons in the nucleus than there are electrons. A positively charged ion is called a **cation**. For example, a sodium atom loses one electron to form a sodium cation of a +1 charge. Using the atomic symbol for sodium we can write $Na \rightarrow e^- + Na^+$.

An atom that gains one or more electrons acquires an excess negative charge and is called an **anion**. Thus, the equation for chlorine is $Cl + e^- \rightarrow Cl^-$.

An ionic compound forms when cations and anions from different elements combine to make an electrically neutral substance. The formula of the compound is written as the lowest whole number ratio of cations and anions that must combine to make an electrically neutral unit. That is why ordinary table salt, sodium chloride, has the formula $NaCl$. Notice that it is standard practice to write the cation symbol first.

Many simple, common ionic compounds are used in everyday life. Potassium chloride, KCl, is a component in salt substitutes for people who must restrict their intake of sodium ions to control high blood pressure. Table salt is normally sold in its "iodized" form; it contains a small amount of NaI or KI (sodium iodide or potassium iodide) to prevent problems with the thyroid gland. In the winter, ice on roads and walkways can be melted with the help of calcium chloride, $CaCl_2$. This ionic compound consists of one Ca^{2+} ion for every two Cl^- ions.

Polyatomic ions contain more than one type of atom acting as a unit with an overall net positive or negative charge. The atoms in the polyatomic ion are joined together by sharing electrons (covalent bonds). Some examples of common polyatomic ions are:

NH_4^+	ammonium	[The ion contains one N atom, 4 H atoms, and has an overall +1 charge.]
HCO_3^-	bicarbonate	[The ion contains 1 H, 1 C, and 3 O atoms and carries a net -1 charge.]
CO_3^{2-}	carbonate	[The ion has 1 C and 3 O atoms with a net charge of -2.]
OH^-	hydroxide	[The ion has a net charge of -1.]
NO_3^-	nitrate	[Each N is joined to 3 O atoms and the ion has a net charge of -1.]
SO_4^{2-}	sulfate	[For each 1 S there are 4 O atoms and the whole ion has a charge of -2.]

Polyatomic ions combine just as simpler ions do: The total + and – charge is balanced out to make a neutral compound. Thus, "baking soda" is sodium bicarbonate, $NaHCO_3$. Laundry detergents often contain "washing soda" or sodium carbonate, Na_2CO_3. Agricultural fertilizers incorporate ammonium nitrate, NH_4NO_3, into their mixtures.

Many ionic compounds dissolve in water, and when they do so, the cations and anions dissociate or separate from each other. An ionic compound dissolved in water has its cations and anions surrounded by a coating of H_2O molecules. Although water is not an ionic compound the distribution of electron density in the molecule is not uniform. As a result, oxygen is a center of negative charge in the molecule and is attracted to cations, while the hydrogens are relatively low in electron density and are attracted to anions.

We can illustrate the interaction of the ions with water by looking at dissolving solid NaCl in water. The process may be described by the equation:

$$NaCl_{(solid)} + H_2O_{(excess\ liquid)} \rightarrow Na^+_{(aquated)} + Cl^-_{(aquated)},$$

where "aquated" means "surrounded by water molecules." Graphically, the dissolving of NaCl in water is represented as

If an ionic compound containing polyatomic ions dissolves in water the anions and cations dissociate; however, the atoms making up the polyatomic ion do not separate from each other. For example, $NaNO_3$ dissolves in water to liberate Na^+ and NO_3^- ions surrounded by a coating of water molecules as shown above for NaCl.

Not all ionic compounds dissolve in water. If water is unable to surround either ion sufficiently enough to overcome the electrostatic attraction between the cation and anion, the ionic compound remains insoluble (or only a miniscule quantity dissolves). In the same way, mixing two solutions of ions will result in the formation of a precipitate if a very strongly attracted cation and anion are brought together.

Background

Scientists often need to identify substances found at a crime scene, materials left in improperly labeled containers, or chemicals in a naturally-occurring mixture. Chemists study the physical and chemical properties of known substances to find characteristics that are useful for identification. In this experiment you will examine solutions of several known ionic compounds, and based upon your observations, determine the identity of an unknown compound chosen from among those already studied.

Many common ionic compounds contain metal cations. Long ago humans discovered that characteristic colors are imparted to a flame when certain metal cations are added to a burning mixture—the beautiful colors of fireworks are accomplished exactly this way. Much later chemists deduced that heat raises the electrons in the metal to a higher energy level in a process called *excitation*. When the excited atoms *relax* or release energy, some of it is emitted as visible light. The color of the light is highly characteristic of the metal being excited by the heat of the flame. Thus, these flame tests are one type of physical property that chemists use to identify metal ions.

Chemists also learned over the years that particular combinations of cations and anions form ionic compounds that are insoluble in water. For example, silver nitrate ($AgNO_3$) dissolves in water to make a colorless solution. This fact indicates that Ag^+ and NO_3^- ions are much more attracted to water molecules than to each other. Sodium chloride (NaCl) and sodium nitrate ($NaNO_3$) also readily dissolve in water. However, when a water solution of $AgNO_3$ is mixed with a solution of $NaCl$, the mixture becomes turbid as a solid separates from the liquid mixture. It is reasonable to conclude that the solid is $AgCl$ and that the solution contains Na^+ and NO_3^- ions. (Why?) Chemists long ago verified that the precipitate is indeed $AgCl$. The following equation describes what happens:

$$AgNO_3\ _{(aq)}\ +\ NaCl\ _{(aq)}\ \rightarrow\ AgCl\ _{(s)}\ +\ NaNO_3\ _{(aq)}\ .$$

Note: the subscript "aq" means the compound is dissolved in water, while
"s" means that compound has precipitated as a solid from solution.

By performing similar experiments with many ionic compounds, it is possible to come up with lists of cation and anion combinations that make insoluble compounds. Suppose a solution is suspected of containing Ag^+. Some aqueous $NaCl$ can be mixed with it, and if a white precipitate forms, it is very possible that Ag^+ or some other ion that makes an insoluble compound with Cl^- is present.

The last example shows us that a single experiment may not be able to uniquely identify a substance. This is why chemists like to use multiple chemical and physical tests to make an identification of an unknown substance. As more tests are performed, it becomes less likely that two different substances would behave exactly the same way in all the tests. In this lab, you will combine the results of flame tests and precipitation reactions to identify an unknown.

Working Safely

The ionic compounds you will be using are not hazardous unless ingested or introduced into your eyes or nose. Wear safety glasses or goggles to prevent solutions from being splashed in your eyes, particularly the basic solutions of sodium hydroxide and sodium carbonate. If any of the solutions is splashed into your eyes, immediately flush them for about 10 minutes at the eye-wash fountain, and then seek medical attention.

Wash off any of the solutions spilled onto your skin with cool water.

Follow your instructor's directions for the proper use of the gas burner. Do not leave the burning flame unattended. Secure loose clothing and long hair to prevent it from coming in contact with the flame.

Your waste solutions should not be flushed down the sink; this may be against local regulations and also will help to prevent the precipitates from clogging the drains. Pour the waste solutions into the container your instructor has provided.

Procedure

Your instructor will provide aqueous solutions of these ionic compounds in dispenser bottles: $LiNO_3$, $MgCl_2$, $CaCl_2$, $SrCl_2$, $NaOH$, Na_2CO_3, KBr, and K_2SO_4. You also will receive an unidentified sample of one of these compounds.

Part 1: Flame Tests

1. You will need 9 cotton-tipped sticks or swabs, a 250-mL beaker half-filled with water, a gas burner, and matches or a striker to light the flame.

2. There are several types of gas burners that are available in chemistry laboratories. Follow your instructor's directions for the correct use of your burner.

3. Light a small gas flame.

4. Take one of the cotton-tipped sticks and moisten the cotton with 3–5 drops of distilled water.

5. Bring the moistened cotton into the upper blue part of the flame. Hold the cotton in the flame for about 10 seconds and observe what color the flame acquires, if any. Immediately place the burning cotton-covered stick in the beaker of water.

6. Record your observation in Table 1 on the Worksheet.

7. Repeat steps 4, 5, and 6 for each of the ionic compounds and the unknown. Use a different clean cotton swab for each solution being tested.

8. Shut off the gas. Take care in handling the burner—the metal parts are hot!

Part 2: Mixing Tests
1. Label four 12-mm x 75-mm test tubes as follows: 11, 12, 13, and 14.

2. Add 10 drops of $LiNO_3$ solution to each tube.

3. Add 10 drops of: NaOH to tube 11; Na_2CO_3 to tube 12; KBr to tube 13; and K_2SO_4 to tube 14.

4. Gently shake or tap each tube to mix the liquids. Examine each tube for the presence or absence of a precipitate and record the result in Table 2 on the Worksheet.

5. If you do not have a total of 16 test tubes available, empty the contents of the four tubes into the waste container and rinse them thoroughly with distilled water.

6. Label four tubes 21, 22, 23, and 24. Add 10 drops of $MgCl_2$ to each tube.

7. Proceed as in step 3, and then repeat steps 4 and 5.

8. Label four tubes 31, 32, 33, and 34. Add 10 drops of $CaCl_2$ to each tube.

9. Proceed as in step 3, and then repeat steps 4 and 5.

10. Label four tubes 41, 42, 43, and 44. Add 10 drops of $SrCl_2$ to each tube.

11. Proceed as in step 3, and then repeat steps 4 and 5.

Part 3: The Unknown
1. You previously performed the flame test on your unknown. Use your result to decide which one of the ionic compounds used in the experiment most likely could be your unknown.
   You might also find it useful to determine which compounds most likely could *not* be your unknown.

2. Select 3 or 4 of the other compounds that could be used in mixing tests with your unknown to provide support for your tentative identification of the unknown. Perform these tests using 10 drops of the unknown and 10 drops of the solution of a known ionic compound, just as in Part 2 above. Record the results in Table 3 on the Worksheet.

Pre-Lab Exercise A
Describe the purpose of the experiment in a few complete sentences of your own phrasing.

Pre-Lab Exercise B
Make a list of the chemicals and equipment you need for this experiment.

Pre-Lab Exercise C
Each of the following ionic compounds dissolves in water. For each formula, write the name of the compound, the formula and charge on the cation, and the formula and charge on the anion.

Formula of Compound	Compound Name	Cation	Anion
KBr	_____	_____	_____
$LiNO_3$	_____	_____	_____
$CaCl_2$	_____	_____	_____
Na_2CO_3	_____	_____	_____
$MgCl_2$	_____	_____	_____
K_2SO_4	_____	_____	_____
$SrCl_2$	_____	_____	_____
NaOH	_____	_____	_____

Pre-Lab Exercise D
A precipitate forms when an aqueous solution of $CaCl_2$ is mixed with a solution of NaF. What is the formula of the precipitate?

Write a reaction equation for what happens.

Pre-Lab Exercise E

What is the precipitate that forms when an aqueous solution of K_2SO_4 is combined with aqueous $Pb(NO_3)_2$? Note: The formula is written this way to show that two NO_3^- ions combine with one Pb^{2+}.

What is the formula of the precipitate?

Write a reaction equation for what happens.

Pre-Lab Exercise F

Fe^{3+} ions and phosphate ions (PO_4^{3-}) combine to make an insoluble compound. What is its formula?

Most ionic compounds containing sodium ions (Na^+) are soluble in water. What is the formula of the water-soluble ionic compound containing sodium and phosphate ions?

Fe^{3+} ion makes a water-soluble ionic compound with chloride ions (Cl^-). What is the formula of this compound?

Write an equation for the reaction between the *soluble* compounds of Fe^{3+} and PO_4^{3-} that makes the *insoluble* compound of Fe^{3+} and PO_4^{3-} . Use the subscript (aq) to denote those compounds found in solution and (s) to identify solids that precipitate from solution.

Lab Worksheet   **Name:** _____   **Section:** _____

1. Record your observations from the flame tests in Table 1 below. The color of the flame when the cotton swab is moistened with distilled water only is used as the reference.
   · If a cotton swab moistened with the solution of the ionic compound produces the same color as water alone, record the result as "none."
   · If the flame acquires a different color when the swab is moistened with the solution of an ionic compound, record the color of the flame.
   · If you cannot determine if the color of the flame has changed by introducing the sample of the ionic compound, repeat the test.
     Write a "?" if you are still unsure about the color after repeating the test.

Table 1: Flame Test Results for Several Ionic Compounds

Compound	Flame Result		Compound	Flame Result
H_2O			NaOH	
$LiNO_3$			Na_2CO_3	
$MgCl_2$			KBr	
$CaCl_2$			K_2SO_4	
$SrCl_2$			Unknown	

2. Record the results of the mixing tests in Table 2 below. Notice that the $LiNO_3$ solution was tested with NaOH, Na_2CO_3, KBr, and K_2SO_4 in that order. Each numbered box in the grid corresponds to a particular combination of two ionic compounds you tested.
   · If the combination of the two solutions produced a precipitate, enter "+" in the box.
   · If the combination of the two solutions formed a cloudy, opaque, or turbid solution, enter "susp" (for *suspension*). This means a solid formed, but the particles may be too small to settle out.
   · If the combination of the two solutions resulted in a clear liquid, enter "NR" in the box for "no reaction."

Table 2: Mixing Tests Results for Several Ionic Compounds

	NaOH	Na_2CO_3	KBr	K_2SO_4
$LiNO_3$	(11)	(12)	(13)	(14)
$MgCl_2$	(21)	(22)	(23)	(24)
$CaCl_2$	(31)	(32)	(33)	(34)
$SrCl_2$	(41)	(42)	(43)	(44)

3. Look back at the flame test results in Table 1. What compound or compounds most likely could be your unknown? Why?

What compounds most likely could not be your unknown? Why?

4. Complete Table 3 below to record the results of the mixing tests you performed with your unknown.

Table 3: Results of Mixing Tests with Unknown

Ionic Compound Mixed with Unknown	Result ‡

‡ Use the same notations as in Table 2: "+" means a precipitate formed,
"susp" means a suspension resulted, and "NR" means no reaction occurred.

5. Based on your results, which compound appears to be your unknown? Explain or justify your conclusion in a few sentences.
If it is not possible to narrow down your conclusion to a single compound, what two compounds most likely could be your unknown? Explain why you cannot distinguish between these two based on your results.

6. Look back at Table 2. Write a reaction equation for each combination of compounds you observed to form a precipitate (marked with a "+"). Include the formulas of the products, and identify which is the solid and which remained in solution using the subscripts (s) and (aq), respectively.

7 Of Alkenes and Vegetables

- Thin Layer Chromatography -

Companion Sections in Waldron: Chapter 3.2, 3.6, and 3.7

Introduction

Compounds containing carbons with double bonds are very common in materials manufactured by plants. Indeed, the color of tomatoes, carrots, squash, pumpkins, yams, and sweet potatoes is the result of several substances that contain very large chains of carbon-carbon double bonds. These materials have the common names lycopene, β-carotene, and xanthophyll; the corresponding bonding arrangements are shown below. These structures use condensed formula notation for single-bonded carbons with two hydrogens (CH_2) or three hydrogens (CH_3).

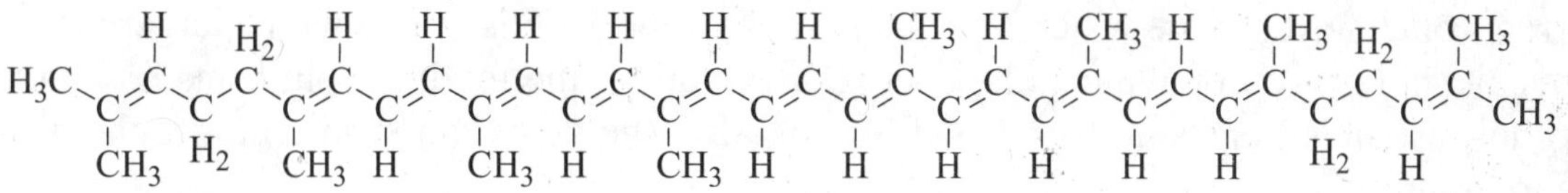

Lycopene

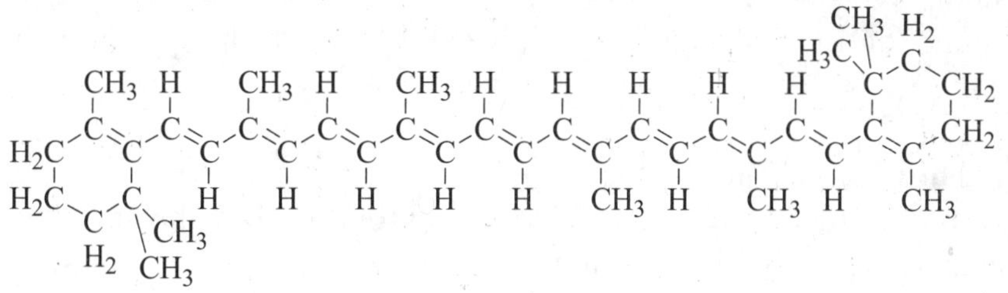

β-Carotene

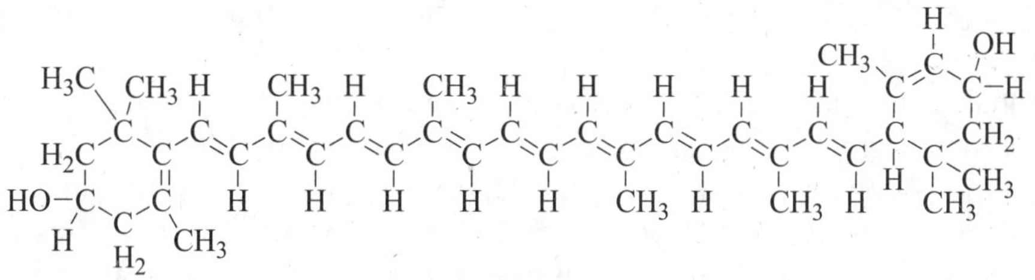

Xanthophyll

Notice that the three compounds all have an extensive set of alternating carbon-carbon double and single bonds. While lycopene is an acyclic molecule (meaning it has no rings of carbon atoms), β-carotene contains two rings of six singly bonded carbons. Xanthophyll is like β-carotene in having two rings of carbons, but each of these rings in turn has one carbon bonded to an alcohol group (a C-OH arrangement).

The structures of lycopene, β-carotene, and xanthophyll may appear complex, but they actually are far less complicated than those of other biological materials. Curiously, these three pigments and many other related compounds are constructed in plant cells, or biosynthesized, from a simple substance related to the alkene *isoprene*:

$$H_2C \overset{}{=} \underset{CH_3}{\overset{}{C}} \text{---} \overset{\overset{H}{|}}{C} \overset{}{=} CH_2$$

In this experiment you will first isolate a mixture containing some or all of these alkenes from tomato paste and pureed carrots (baby food) or several other possible sources. Using the technique of *thin layer chromatography* (TLC for short) you will be able to determine how many alkenes are present in each mixture; the color of the pigments and some deductive reasoning will help you identify each alkene.

Background: Isolation of the Pigments

Plant and animal tissues consist largely of water. Even though tomato paste contains much less water than fresh tomatoes, a significant amount of moisture remains. Pureed carrots contain even more water. When a portion of the food is mixed with a larger volume of ethyl alcohol or isopropyl alcohol, water is drawn out of the food; the pigments remain in the alcohol-insoluble vegetable tissue. A filtration after the dehydration to removes the alcohol-water mixture.

The lycopene, β-carotene, and xanthophyll easily dissolve in solvents with properties like those of hydrocarbons, while the larger molecules making up the tissue do not dissolve. Once again, a filtration separates the desired pigments from the waste solids. The solution or *extract* containing the pigments is then freed of the last traces of water, concentrated by evaporating some of the solvent, and analyzed by the technique known as *thin layer chromatography*.

Background: Thin Layer Chromatography

At some point you probably have seen or participated in the sporting event called a "race." The contestants start, clumped together, from the same point or starting line. When the race begins each participant typically runs forward as fast as possible; after a while, the individual racers begin to pull apart or separate from one another. If all the runners stopped at the exact moment the winner reached the finish line, each would hold a position on the track that reflected how fast each was traveling. In effect, we could rank or rate each athlete according to speed.

In an analogous way, the components of a mixture can be separated by the technique of thin layer chromatography (TLC). A flat plate of glass or plastic about the size of a microscope slide is coated with a very finely divided solid such as aluminum oxide or silica (among others possibilities). This layer of solid is only a millimeter or so thick on the glass or plastic sheet. A solution containing the mixture of compounds to be analyzed is applied as a small drop near one edge of the plate. The small volume of solvent quickly evaporates from the plate leaving the compounds to be separated as a residue clinging to the surface of the solid on the plate, as shown in Figure 7-1(a).

The "race" begins when the plate is dipped into a small puddle of solvent just below the level of the residue clinging to the plate, as shown in Figure 7-1(b). As the solvent "creeps" or climbs up the plate some of the components dissolve in the liquid and travel up the plate; some of the other compounds in the mixture, which are more attracted to the solid surface, lag behind. If the level of the liquid is allowed to travel up the plate far enough, the individual components in the mixture are teased apart with each at a different distance from the original spot of residue as indicated in Figure 7-1(c).

In an ideal thin layer chromatography experiment each of the compounds in the mixture moves up the plate at a different speed because of the difference in attraction for the solvent and the solid on the plate. When the compounds are colored each individual component appears as a separate "spot" or "dot" on the plate at the end of the solvent travel time. Thus, the number of spots indicates how many components were in the mixture. If each component has a unique, identifiable color then it is possible to tell which compound is found in each spot.

You might wonder what factors control how far different compounds travel on a chromatography plate. The short answer is that compounds differ in their attraction to the solvent and the solid on the surface of the plate. Any compound attracted to the plate surface more strongly than to the solvent will tend to move very little. In contrast, any compound that has little affinity for the plate surface will tend to be swept along with the solvent moving up the plate. These attractive forces can be related to the structure of the organic compounds being separated. For example, compounds having an C-O-H grouping like xanthophyll generally have stronger attraction to the silica gel on the TLC plate than compounds such as β-carotene and lycopene, which lack the oxygen-containing group. (The relationship between structure and chemical/physical properties is very important in organic and biological chemistry. You will hear more about this topic later in the course.)

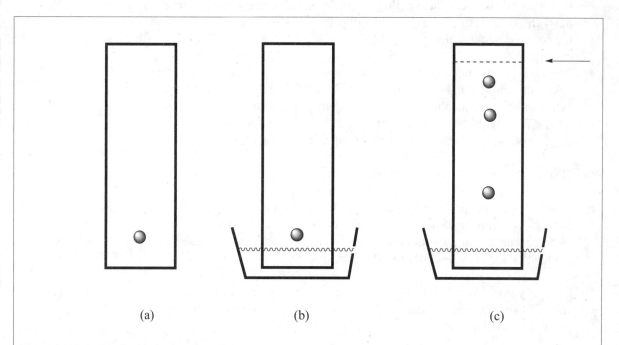

(a)   (b)   (c)

Figure 7-1: A thin layer chromatography experiment
 (a) Thin layer chromatography plate with a sample of mixture deposited on it near one edge.
 (b) The plate is dipped into a solvent below the level of the mixture to prevent "flushing" the sample away; the solvent creeps up the plate surface by capillary attraction.
 (c) By the time the solvent has traveled to the level indicated by the arrow, the individual components of the original mixture have been separated as each travels up the plate to a different extent with the solvent.

> **Working Safely**
>
> This experiment uses ethyl or isopropyl alcohol and ethyl acetate as solvents. These liquids are volatile and flammable. Use them in a hood or a well-ventilated area away from any open flames. Avoid prolonged inhalation of their vapors or contact with your skin. Your instructor may have gloves for you to use. Any excess or waste solvents should be placed in the container set aside for disposal. Be sure to wear safety glasses or goggles!

Hint: The experiment is easier to do if you work with one or two partners who isolate pigment from a different food source. By sharing pigment extracts each partner can analyze two or three different pigment samples on his or her own TLC plate. [Your instructor may choose to have the partners prepare just one plate.] Tomato paste and pureed carrots (baby food) are very good sources of the pigments. You may also want to investigate condensed tomato soup, catsup, pureed yams or sweet potatoes, and pumpkin as sources of the pigments.

Procedure

Reminders

1. Weigh out 5–6 g of food into a 100-mL beaker.

    —

2. Add 10 mL of 95% ethyl alcohol or isopropyl alcohol to the food in the beaker. Stir the mixture together for several minutes until the texture of the food no longer seems to be changing.

    Alcohol is flammable; avoid inhalation of the vapors or absorption through your skin.

3. Support a short-stem funnel on a rack or iron ring with the stem draining into a 50-mL beaker. Place a plug of cotton (about the size of a cosmetic puff) in the bottom of the funnel to trap the food particles. Do not push the cotton down into the stem.

    —

4. Press the cotton plug with a spatula down into the bottom of the funnel to cover the outlet, and pour the food-alcohol mixture into the funnel. When most of the alcohol has drained into the small beaker, press down on the food with the back side of a plastic spoon or the broad face of a large cork. Squeeze out as much of the liquid as reasonably possible.

5. Discard the alcohol into a container marked "waste alcohol."

    —

    Ethyl acetate is also flammable. Its vapors are irritating to inhale, and it can be absorbed through skin. Gloves are recommended here!

6. Transfer the food paste (with or without the cotton) to another small, dry beaker. Working in a hood or a well-ventilated area, add 8–10 mL of ethyl acetate to the food and stir the mixture together with a glass rod or wood stick for a few minutes to extract the pigments.

    —

7. Carefully pour the ethyl acetate extract of the pigments into a 10- or 25-mL Erlenmeyer flask, leaving the food solids in the beaker. (This technique is called *decantation*.)

    —

    Local/state regulations may prohibit disposal of the food waste in the trash.

8. Dump the food residue into a waste container provided by your instructor.

    —

9. Insert a wood stick or splint into the Erlenmeyer flask so that it dips into the ethyl acetate extract of the pigment. Place the flask on an electric hot plate in a hood or a well-ventilated area. Evaporate ethyl acetate over low heat until the volume has been reduced to about 1–2 mL. The stick will help moderate the boiling. The evaporation occurs quickly, so do not leave your flask unattended.

    WARNING: Do not evaporate ethyl acetate near any flames. Do not use a gas burner to heat the ethyl acetate.

10. Remove the flask from the hot plate and let it cool briefly to room temperature. Stopper the flask and set it aside.

11. Obtain a 3- x 10-cm silica gel TLC plate from your instructor. Handle the plate by the edges to avoid transfer of skin oils to the plate. The side coated with the white powder is used for the thin layer chromatography analysis.

12. Very gently draw a pencil line about 0.5 cm away from and parallel to one 3-cm edge of the plate. This is the "starting line." Draw another line to mark the "finish" about 1 cm away from the other narrow edge of the plate. Do not dig a "trench" in the surface of the silica gel by pressing down too hard on the plate with the pencil tip.

13. Your instructor will provide you with a very fine glass capillary tube to transfer some of each extract to the starting line of the plate. Dip the tip of the capillary into the ethyl acetate pigment extract, and some of the liquid will be drawn up into the tube. When you gently and briefly touch the tip of the capillary to a point on the starting line of the silica gel plate, some of the liquid will be transferred to the plate. Keep the capillary tip in contact with the plate very briefly—only long enough to make a spot smaller than 3 mm in diameter. The solvent evaporates quickly. Repeat the application of the extract two or three more times *in the very same place* on the plate, keeping the spot diameter about 3 mm or less.

—

See Figure 7-2 for the placement of pigment samples on the starting line of the thin layer plate. Two or three different pigments can be placed on the same chromatography plate.

—

14. Repeat step 13 for one or two more pigment samples as shown in Figure 7-2. Set the plate aside while you prepare the chromatography chamber.

15. The chromatography experiment takes place when liquid moves up the plate by capillary attraction. Measure out 5 mL of the developing solvent (10–15% ethyl acetate by volume in hexane) in a dry 10-mL graduated cylinder and transfer it to a 250-mL beaker or a small bottle. Cover and seal the beaker with aluminum foil or close the bottle with a screw cap. Allow the container to stand for about 5 minutes so that the air inside is saturated with the solvent vapors—this helps keep the solvent from evaporating off the plate during the chromatography experiment.

16. Pick up the thin layer plate with a pair of tweezers above the "finish line." Gently lower the plate down into the solvent so that the liquid level is below the starting line when the edge of the plate rests on the bottom of the container. Reseal the beaker or bottle.

17. Watch what happens as the liquid climbs up the plate surface. When the liquid level reaches the "finish line," open the container and remove the plate with the tweezers. Allow the plate to air dry briefly. If you will not be using the solvent to develop another plate, place it in the container for the flammable waste.

18. Use a pencil to draw a circle around the colored spots that appear on the chromatography plate. Be sure to observe and record the colors before the pigments fade from exposure to air.

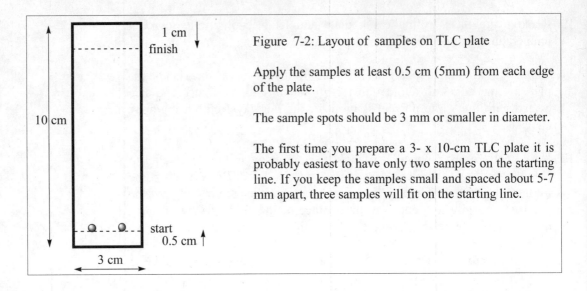

Figure 7-2: Layout of samples on TLC plate

Apply the samples at least 0.5 cm (5mm) from each edge of the plate.

The sample spots should be 3 mm or smaller in diameter.

The first time you prepare a 3- x 10-cm TLC plate it is probably easiest to have only two samples on the starting line. If you keep the samples small and spaced about 5-7 mm apart, three samples will fit on the starting line.

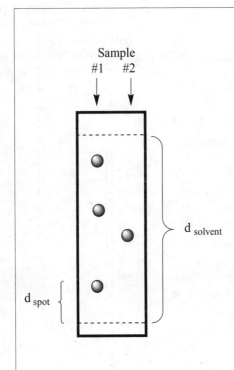

Figure 7-3: A developed TLC plate

Two substances to be analyzed originally were deposited on the starting line, and then the solvent was allowed to travel up the plate.

Three spots are seen in the vertical "track" or "lane" for Sample #1. This means there are at least three substances in the mixture placed on the starting line.

Only one spot appears in the lane for Sample #2. This suggests that the sample was pure, or contained only one substance.

The R_f (ratio-to-front) value for each spot on a developed plate is a fraction that is calculated as the distance a spot travels from the starting line, d_{spot}, divided by the distance the solvent moved, $d_{solvent}$. Thus, for the lowest spot in the lane for Sample #1, $R_f = d_{spot}/d_{solvent}$. Distances are all measured in mm or cm.

A compound that is not highly attracted to the TLC plate travels along with the solvent and has an R_f closer to 1, while a compound that clings to the surface of the plate more tightly moves little and has an R_f closer to 0.

The distance a spot travels is measured from the starting line to the top edge of the spot.

Pre-Lab Exercise A
Describe the purpose of the experiment in a few complete sentences of your own phrasing.

Pre-Lab Exercise B
Make a list of the chemicals and equipment you need for this experiment.

Pre-Lab Exercise C
What are the molecular formulas of lycopene, β-carotene, and xanthophyll?
How many units of isoprene are used by a plant to synthesize the carbon backbone of each pigment?

Pre-Lab Exercise D
Choose one of the pigments and draw a circle around each segment of the compound derived from a single molecule of isoprene. There should be a whole number of isoprene units needed to make the entire pigment!

Pre-Lab Exercise E
Explain why the electrons in the carbon-carbon double bonds of the pigments are considered to be "delocalized."

Pre-Lab Exercise F

Suppose you are working in a crime lab and need to determine if a white powder found on a suspect was cocaine or only powdered aspirin. How could you use thin layer chromatography to answer the question? What specific information would you be looking for to make a decision in this case? Assume that you have pure samples of cocaine and aspirin available for reference.

Pre-Lab Exercise G

Explain how solvent is able to travel "up" a thin layer chromatography plate in apparent defiance of gravity.

Pre-Lab Exercise H

Why must the spots of samples on the "starting line" of a thin layer chromatography plate be above the level of the solvent at the very start of the separation experiment?

What would happen if the TLC plate were "dunked" under the surface of the liquid when the experiment was started?

Lab Worksheet   **Name:** _____   **Section:** _____

1. Several blank TLC plates are represented below. On plate A sketch an accurate drawing of the developed plate containing samples of tomato paste and pureed carrots that shows the location and color of any spots you saw.

    Use blank plates B and C to sketch the developed thin layer chromatography plates from other foods you investigated.

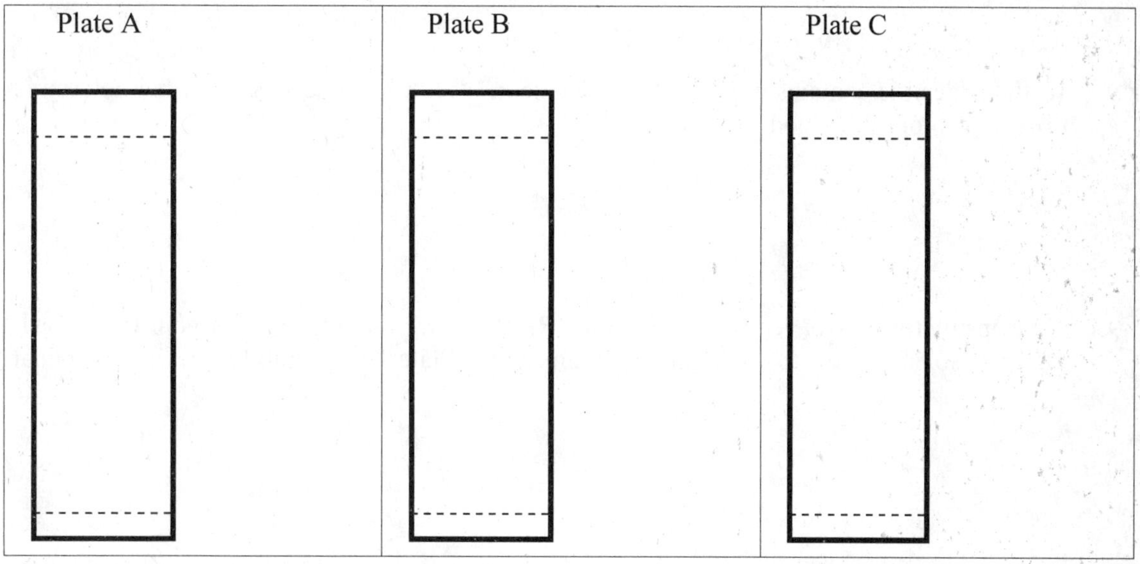

Plate A	Plate B	Plate C

2. How many pigments appear to be found in tomato paste? In pureed carrots? Why?

3. The dominant pigment in carrots is β-carotene, while in tomatoes lycopene is dominant. Based on this information, identify the location of the β-carotene and lycopene spots on Plate A.

4. If xanthophyll is more attracted to the TLC plate than either β-carotene or lycopene, where would it show up on Plate A relative to the spots for the other two pigments?

5. Which pigment is more highly attracted to the silica gel on the surface of the plate: β-carotene or lycopene? What experimental result demonstrates this?

6. Do carrots and tomatoes have any pigments in common? What are they?

7. Looking at Plates B and C, what other foods contain:
   lycopene?

   β-carotene?

   xanthophyll?

8. If the vegetable contains more than one pigment, offer a hypothesis about what determines the observed color of the food.

9. Your instructor may have you calculate the R_f values for the pigments on your developed TLC plates. If so, show how to do that for the pigments on Plate A. Refer to Figure 7-3 for guidance.

10. What general statement can you make about the size of a spot's R_f value and the compound's attraction to the silica gel on the plate?

11. Does the same compound (lycopene, β-carotene, or xanthophyll) have the same R_f on different silica plates developed with the same solvent mixture? How might you use this observation to identify materials by TLC?

Companion Sections in Waldron: Chapters 3.6, 3.7, and 3.8

Introduction

Humans have made and used tools throughout our race's existence. Some tools are physical objects to make a job easier like a saw, hammer, or wheelbarrow. People also make models—conceptual tools that help make sense of the world by explaining how things "fit" together or work. For example, the common expressions "the sun rises" and "the sun sets" are models to explain how the sun appears to change position relative to Earth each day, even though the sun does not move about the planet. Models can also be physical representations of real objects on a different order of scale that make it easier to understand. Thus, a globe is a model of the surface of Earth; many of us have assembled small models of airplanes and automobiles.

Science has a model for understanding the inner workings of atoms called *atomic theory*, which describes an atom as an incomprehensibly small ball of positively charged and uncharged particles (protons and neutrons, respectively) surrounded by a very large volume of mostly empty space occupied by an equal number of negatively charged particles (electrons).

The *Periodic Table* of the elements organizes what scientists know about the mass and number of electrons in each atom. Those elements with the same number of electrons available for bonding are arranged in the same column or group.

Atoms assemble themselves into larger electrically neutral substances called molecules. Long before good models were developed to explain *how* atoms join together to make molecules, scientists needed to show *what* the connections were among atoms in a molecule. One of the more common ways to do so is still in use: Chemists write the atomic symbol for the elements and join the atoms by lines to show the bonds. For example, water is often written H—O—H to show that the oxygen atom is connected to two hydrogen atoms that are not connected to each other.

In the 1920s Professor Gilbert N. Lewis (of the University of California, Berkley) suggested that lines connecting atoms were actually a pair of electrons in a region of space between two nuclei. Essentially the two nuclei play a game of tug of war for the electron pair, but neither nucleus wins and neither quits playing the game! As a result, both atoms are bonded together by their mutual attraction for the same electrons.

Professor Lewis' proposition made it possible for chemists to use atomic theory and the Periodic Table to predict structures for compounds based on their formula. Lewis recognized that several elements commonly found in living organisms—carbon, nitrogen, oxygen, sulfur, phosphorous—as well as fluorine, chlorine, bromine, and iodine could have as many as four pairs of electrons (i.e., eight total) at the outermost energy level. Hydrogen, having a single electron of its own, can at most have one pair in its outer energy level.

In Lewis' model for bonding the symbol for an element is surrounded by up to four pairs of "dots" equal to the number of electrons it has available to use for bonding. (Hydrogen can have two electrons at most.) Single electrons are those available for pairing up in a covalent bond, while the two electrons in a pair typically remain unshared.

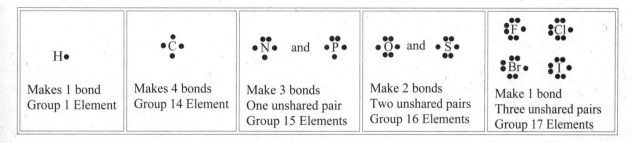

H•	•C•	•N• and •P•	•O• and •S•	•F• •Cl• •Br• •I•
Makes 1 bond Group 1 Element	Makes 4 bonds Group 14 Element	Make 3 bonds One unshared pair Group 15 Elements	Make 2 bonds Two unshared pairs Group 16 Elements	Make 1 bond Three unshared pairs Group 17 Elements

You can draw a plausible model for the structure of a compound using the molecular formula and the Lewis structures of the elements. Thus, the common materials water (H_2O), natural gas (CH_4), and ammonia (NH₃) can be represented with the Lewis structures shown below. The corresponding structures using a dash for a covalent bond are also given.

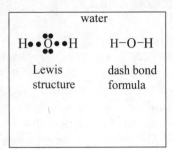

water

H••Ö••H   H–O–H

Lewis   dash bond
structure   formula

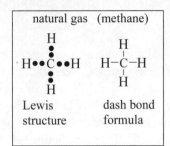

natural gas (methane)

H••C••H   H–C–H

Lewis   dash bond
structure   formula

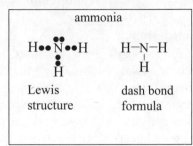

ammonia

H••N••H   H–N–H

Lewis   dash bond
structure   formula

Lewis or dash formulas of compounds are convenient, but they do not tell the whole story about a structure. These drawings demonstrate connections between the atoms in two dimensions while molecules are three-dimensional objects.

Valence shell electron repulsion (or VSEPR) theory gives us a model to predict the actual shape of a molecule in three dimensions. Briefly stated, VSEPR theory says that all the electron *pairs* in different bonds or unshared pairs around an atom repel each other. Consequently, the electron pairs move as far apart in space as possible to minimize the repulsion of like charges. The nuclei of the atoms sharing the electron pairs also distribute themselves to maximize the distance between groups. As a result, we can predict the position in space of bonded atoms by considering how far apart the electron pairs need to be to minimize electrical repulsion.

Chemists sometimes draw simple three-dimensional pictures of molecules, but it is often convenient to describe the geometry or shape of a molecule in terms of bond angles and words. The *bond angle* is the separation in degrees between different bonds made to the same atom. Thus, two bonds can be oriented at angle of 180° around a common atom and three bonds are arranged at 120° angles. Four electron pairs are separated by 109°. The corresponding geometry can also be named.

Two electron pairs are spaced 180° apart around atom X. Electron pair geometry is *linear*.

Three electron pairs are spread out around atom Y so that any two pairs are 120° apart. Electron pair geometry is *trigonal planar*.

Four electron pairs spread out around Z so that any two pairs are spaced 109° apart. Electron pair geometry is *tetrahedral*.

In summary, a simple model for predicting the three-dimensional shape of a molecule around an atom consists of these steps:

1) Use the molecular formula to decide how many atoms of each element are needed to "build" the compound.
2) Use the Periodic Table to construct the Lewis symbol for each atom.
3) Build a Lewis structure for the compound.
4) Determine how far apart the electron pairs around an atom need to be in three dimensions to minimize repulsions.
5) Describe the arrangement of the bonded atoms in space (the "molecular geometry") that share those electrons.

A bit more needs to be said about step (5). If all the electron pairs around an atom are in bonds, the molecular geometry can be described by the same term that describes the arrangement of electron pairs in space. Look back at the Lewis structure for natural gas or methane. The carbon atom is surrounded by four electron pairs pushing away from each other to be separated by angles of 109°. Electrons have too little mass to be detected. On the other hand, the nuclei of atoms contain all the protons and any neutrons in the atom, and each of these particles weighs about 2000 times more than one electron. Scientists *can* detect the location of the nuclei of atoms in space. Thus, the carbon atom in methane appears to be surrounded by four points of mass that are also at 109° angles. We say the molecular geometry of methane is tetrahedral as well.

Now look back at the Lewis structure for water. The oxygen atom is surrounded by four electron pairs, similar to the carbon of methane. These electron pairs push away from each other to about 109°. Unlike methane, only two of the electron pairs around oxygen are shared (i.e., are in bonds). If we were to describe the location of the oxygen and two hydrogen nuclei in space, they would appear to make a "V" or "bent" shape like so:

$$H \diagdown \overset{O}{} \diagup H$$

Thus, the molecular shape of water is "bent" while the electron pair geometry is described as tetrahedral.

In this paper lab you will work with formulas, Lewis structures, and physical molecular model kits to help you better visualize the connections between the common ways the structures of molecules are presented and the actual three-dimensional shape.

Pre-Lab Exercise A

The names and formulas for several common compounds are given below. Also shown is an incomplete Lewis structure for the compound—the arrangement of the atoms is given, but the shared and unshared pairs of electrons are missing. Complete the Lewis structure for each compound, *assuming that only single bonds are present* between atoms. Last, draw the corresponding structure that shows bonds as dashes or lines.

Example Propane, a common fuel C_3H_8	H H H H C C C H H H H incomplete structure	H H H • • • H••C••C••C••H • • • H H H completed Lewis structure	H H H | | | H—C—C—C—H | | | H H H dash formula

a) "Freon-21," Refrigerant gas $CHCl_2F$	Cl H C F Cl Lewis structure	Cl H C F Cl dash formula

	Lewis structure	dash formula
b) "Rubbing alcohol" or "isopropyl alcohol" C_3H_8O	``` H H O H H C C C H H H H ``` Lewis structure	``` H H O H H C C C H H H H ``` dash formula

	Lewis structure	dash formula
c) "MTBE," gasoline additive $C_5H_{12}O$	``` H H H C H H H H C C O C H H H H C H H H ``` Lewis structure	``` H H H C H H H H C C O C H H H H C H H H ``` dash formula

	Lewis structure	dash formula
d) "Isopropyl amine," solvent C_3H_9N	``` H H H N H H C C C H H H H ``` Lewis structure	``` H H H N H H C C C H H H H ``` dash formula

Pre-Lab Exercise B

Complete the Lewis structure for these compounds, each of which contains one or more double bonds as indicated. Then draw the corresponding structure that shows bonds as dashes or lines.

	Lewis structure	dash formula
a) "MEK," solvent C_4H_8O (one C, O double bond)	``` H O H H H C C C C H H H H ``` Lewis structure	``` H O H H H C C C C H H H H ``` dash formula

b) Propylene, used to make plastic C_3H_6 (one C, C double bond)	$\begin{array}{ccc} \text{H} & & \text{H} \\ \text{H} \ \text{C} & \text{C} & \text{C} \ \text{H} \\ & \text{H} & \text{H} \end{array}$ Lewis structure	$\begin{array}{ccc} \text{H} & & \text{H} \\ \text{H} \ \text{C} & \text{C} & \text{C} \ \text{H} \\ & \text{H} & \text{H} \end{array}$ dash formula

c) Acrylic acid, used to make plastic $C_3H_4O_2$ (one C, C double bond & one C, O double bond)	$\begin{array}{cccc} \text{H} & & \text{O} \\ \text{H} \ \text{C} & \text{C} & \text{C} & \text{O} \ \text{H} \\ & \text{H} \end{array}$ Lewis structure	$\begin{array}{cccc} \text{H} & & \text{O} \\ \text{H} \ \text{C} & \text{C} & \text{C} & \text{O} \ \text{H} \\ & \text{H} \end{array}$ dash formula

Pre-Lab Exercise C

Complete the Lewis structure for these compounds, each of which contains a triple bond as indicated. Then draw the corresponding structure that shows bonds as dashes or lines.

a) Butyne, industrial gas C_4H_6	$\begin{array}{ccccc} \text{H} & \text{H} \\ \text{H} \ \text{C} & \text{C} & \text{C} & \text{C} \ \text{H} \\ \text{H} & \text{H} \end{array}$ Lewis structure	$\begin{array}{ccccc} \text{H} & \text{H} \\ \text{H} \ \text{C} & \text{C} & \text{C} & \text{C} \ \text{H} \\ \text{H} & \text{H} \end{array}$ dash formula

b) Acrylonitrile, used to make plastic C_3H_3N (contains C, N triple bond & a C, C double bond)	$\begin{array}{ccccc} \text{N} & \text{C} & \text{C} & \text{C} & \text{H} \\ & & \text{H} & \text{H} \end{array}$ Lewis structure	$\begin{array}{ccccc} \text{N} & \text{C} & \text{C} & \text{C} & \text{H} \\ & & \text{H} & \text{H} \end{array}$ dash formula

Pre-Lab Exercise D

Each of the following compounds contains a ring of carbon atoms and several other types of bonds. Use the information provided to complete the Lewis structure and the dash formula for each substance.

a) Salicylic acid, used to make aspirin $C_7H_6O_3$ (contains a ring of 6 carbon atoms with 3 double bonds between carbons)	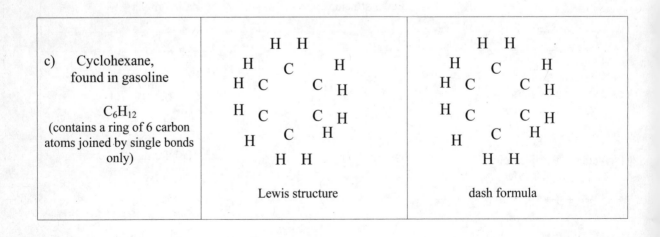H$\quad$O C H$\quad$C$\quad$C$\quad$C$\quad$O$\quad$H H$\quad$C$\quad\quad$C C$\quad\quad$O H$\quad\quad$H Lewis structure	H$\quad$O C H$\quad$C$\quad$C$\quad$C$\quad$O$\quad$H H$\quad$C$\quad\quad$C C$\quad\quad$O H$\quad\quad$H dash formula
b) Methyl anthranilate, artificial grape flavor $C_8H_9NO_2$ (contains a ring of 6 carbon atoms with 3 double bonds between carbons)	H$\quad$O C H$\quad$C$\quad$C$\quad$C$\quad$O$\quad$C$\quad$H H$\quad$C$\quad\quad$C$\quad$N$\quad$H C$\quad\quad$H H Lewis structure	H$\quad$O C H$\quad$C$\quad$C$\quad$C$\quad$O$\quad$C$\quad$H H$\quad$C$\quad\quad$C$\quad$N$\quad$H C$\quad\quad$H H dash formula
c) Cyclohexane, found in gasoline C_6H_{12} (contains a ring of 6 carbon atoms joined by single bonds only)	H$\quad$H H$\quad$C$\quad$H H$\quad$C$\quad\quad$C$\quad$H H$\quad$C$\quad\quad$C$\quad$H H$\quad$C$\quad$H H$\quad$H Lewis structure	H$\quad$H H$\quad$C$\quad$H H$\quad$C$\quad\quad$C$\quad$H H$\quad$C$\quad\quad$C$\quad$H H$\quad$C$\quad$H H$\quad$H dash formula

Lab Worksheet   **Name:** _____   **Section:** _____

In this part of the exercise you are going to assemble three-dimensional models of the compounds used in the Pre-Lab Exercises. (Or, your instructor may have some pre-assembled for you to examine.) There are several types of kits available, so pay particular attention to your lab instructor's advice on how to use them. Most kits use different colors for each type of atom. For example, carbon is often black, oxygen is red, hydrogen is white, and nitrogen is blue. The pieces fit together to show the approximately correct angle between electron pairs.

1. Examine a model of Freon-21. How is the geometry of the electron pairs and atoms around carbon like that found in methane?

    What is similar about the bonding of hydrogen, chlorine, and fluorine atoms?

    What is different about the arrangement of electron pairs around chlorine and fluorine compared with hydrogen?

2. Compare the models of isopropyl alcohol and isopropyl amine. Is there any difference in the arrangement of the electron pairs around oxygen and nitrogen?

    What words describe the arrangement of the electron pairs around oxygen in isopropyl alcohol?

    What words describe the arrangement of the electron pairs around nitrogen in isopropyl amine?

    Why are different words needed to describe the geometry of the atoms bonded to oxygen and nitrogen in these two compounds?

3. Now compare the models of isopropyl alcohol and MTBE.   Why can we say that the electron pair geometry and the molecular geometry around oxygen is the same in these two compounds?

4. Now turn your attention to the models of MEK, propylene, and acrylic acid. What is the approximate bond angle around the double-bonded carbon in each of these compounds?

How many electron pairs appear to be pushing away from each other around the carbon atoms in the C=C or C=O bonds?

5. Examine the Lewis structures and models of butyne and acrylonitrile. What is the bond angle around the carbon(s) in the triple bonds?

   How many pairs of electrons appear to be pushing away or repelling each other?

6. Compare the 6-carbon ring in salicylic acid, methyl anthranilate, and cyclohexane (Pre-Lab Exercise D). What is different about the ring in cyclohexane compared with the other two compounds?

   Based on the structural formula and three-dimensional models, what do you think explains the difference about the rings in cyclohexane and salicylic acid or methyl anthranilate?

7. Consider any of the compounds that contain carbon-carbon double bonds (C=C). Including these two carbons, how many atoms lie in the same plane (flat surface)?

   Why is correct to say that carbon-carbon double bonds have two "faces" or "sides"?

8. Based on what you have learned in this exercise, what type of structure do you expect to be most rigid: a chain of carbons connected by single bonds only; a chain of carbons connected by alternating double and single bonds; or a chain of carbons connected by alternating triple and single bonds? Why?

9. A dash structure for a compound similar to the common pain reliever ibuprofen is shown at the right:

   Using what you have learned in this exercise, predict:
   a) which regions of the compound are flat;

Ibuprofen relative

   b) what the actual bond angles are around the carbon atoms. You can indicate these on the drawing above.

Companion Sections in Waldron: Chapters 4.3 and 5.3

Introduction

Processes that can occur in a forward and reverse direction by the same pathway are called *reversible*. For example, liquid water becomes ice (solid H_2O) at 0° C and ice melts at 0° C: The same H_2O molecules can pass through repeated cycles of freezing and melting as heat flows out of the water or the same amount of heat flows into the ice.

On the other hand, some processes are irreversible. Thus, gasoline ignited in air burns to produce water and carbon dioxide. On the other hand, water and carbon dioxide *cannot* be ignited under the same conditions to produce gasoline.

Imagine that compounds A and B react in a 1:1 ratio to make compounds Y and Z in a 1:1 ratio. The chemical equation that describes the reaction could be written A + B → Y + Z. Suppose we mix compounds A and B and allow them to react. Over time, the amount of A and B will decrease, while the amount of Y and Z in the mixture increases.

If the reaction of A and B to make Y and Z is reversible, then the reverse reaction could be written Y + Z → A + B. This means that if we mix Y and Z under the same conditions used to react A and B, the amount of Y and Z will decrease over time and the amount of A and B in the mixture will increase.

Chemists show that a reaction is reversible by writing the equation like this: A + B ⇆ Y + Z. The forward reaction is the one indicated by reading the equation from left to right; the reverse reaction is found by reading the equation from right to left.

Now here is where things get interesting. If we mix A and B, let them react to make Y and Z, soon enough Y and Z begin reacting to make A and B. After enough time goes by, the speed at which A and B react to make Y and Z exactly matches the speed at which Y and Z react to make A and B. That is, the speed of the forward and reverse reactions become equal. At this point, it appears that the relative amounts of A, B, Y and Z in the mixture do not change: The reaction has reached *equilibrium*. The speed of the forward and reverse reactions are exactly balanced.

When a reaction reaches equilibrium, the amounts of the compounds on both sides of the reaction arrow (⇆) are not necessarily the same. Equilibrium does not mean equal! The mixture of reactants and products may contain overwhelming amounts of products, or it may be heavily concentrated in reactants, or the mixture may consist of any proportion of materials between these extremes. The exact balance of products to reactants at equilibrium must be determined by experiment.

Let's go back to the hypothetical reaction A + B ⇆ Y + Z. Suppose that you mix 1 mole of A and 2 moles of B in a flask at the start of lab—no Y or Z are present—and the reaction begins. Further imagine that you come back every hour and analyze the mixture without having to remove any reactants or products, and prepare a table of your measurements. After several hours this might be what your results looked like:

Time	Moles A	Moles B	Moles Y	Moles Z
Start	1.00	2.00	0	0
1 hour later	0.80	1.80	0.20	0.20
2 hours later	0.70	1.70	0.30	0.30
3 hours later	0.65	1.65	0.35	0.35
5 hours later	0.63	1.63	0.37	0.37
8 hours later	0.63	1.63	0.37	0.37
12 hours later	0.63	1.63	0.37	0.37

Notice that the reaction gradually slowed down as A and B reacted until sometime between 3 and 5 hours later the amounts of A, B, Y, and Z in the mixture ceased to change: The reaction reached equilibrium. In this example, the mixture contained more reactants than products at equilibrium.

Reactions at equilibrium can be disturbed by the addition or removal of any component in the mixture. When this happens, the chemical reaction occurs in whichever direction (forward or reverse) that restores the system to the equilibrium balance. Again, look at the reaction $A + B \leftrightarrows Y + Z$. If we were able to selectively remove Z from the mixture, more A and B would react to make more Y and replace some of the Z. Chemists say the reaction would "shift to the right," or occur in the forward direction. The reaction would come to equilibrium when the balance between products and reactants was restored, though the amounts of the materials would no longer be the same at equilibrium. Here is another example: If A were removed from the equilibrium mixture, reaction would "shift to the left," or occur in the reverse direction. This means some Y and Z would react to produce some A and more B until equilibrium was restored.

Many of the reactions that occur in living cells are reversible. This is advantageous because it allows a living system to respond to stresses and changes that either reduce the amount of reactants available or remove products from the cell.

Background

Iron(III) nitrate, $Fe(NO_3)_3$, dissolves in water to produce a solution containing Fe^{+3} and NO^{-3} ions. The Fe^{+3} ions give the solution a pale yellow color.

Sodium salicylate, $NaC_7H_6O_3$, dissolves in water giving a solution of Na^+ and $C_7H_6O_3^-$ (salicylate) ions. For simplicity, we will represent the $C_7H_6O_3^-$ ions as Sal^-. The solution of Na^+ and Sal^- is colorless.

When solutions of $Fe(NO_3)$ and $NaC_7H_6O_3$ are mixed, the Fe^{+3} and Sal^- ions react to make a reddish-purple material having the formula $[FeSal]^{+2}$. (The brackets are used to show that one Fe^{+3} and one Sal^- are combined to make a new ion with a total charge of +2.) The purple color must come from $[FeSal]^{+2}$ because solutions containing only Na^+ and NO^{-3} are colorless.

An equation for this reaction can be written as $Fe^{+3} + Sal^- \leftrightarrows [FeSal]^{+2}$. The Na^+ and NO^{-3} ions are not shown on either side of the arrows because once the $Fe(NO_3)_3$ and NaSal dissolve in water, the Na^+ and NO^{-3} remain dissociated and unchanged in solution. These ions simply keep the solution electrically neutral by balancing the total positive and negative charge.

The reaction between Fe^{+3} and Sal^- is fast and reversible. As soon as the chemicals are mixed, the reaction comes to equilibrium. Because only the product $[FeSal]^{+2}$ is colored, the intensity of color in the solution indicates how much of the product is present. This gives us a convenient way to examine what factors influence the equilibrium in this reaction. Using it as an example, we can deduce information about other reversible reactions.

Working Safely

None of the chemicals being used in this experiment are toxic unless ingested in significant quantities. Wear safety glasses or goggles to protect your eyes from splashes. The colored substance formed by reaction of the sodium salicylate and iron nitrate may stain your fingers, so it is a good idea to wear gloves. If that is not possible, wash spills off your skin right away. Any discoloration will fade within a day or two of normal washing.

The sodium phosphate solution is basic (alkaline) and the HCl is acidic. Keep your fingers out of your eyes, ears, nose, and mouth to avoid irritation. If you do accidentally get any of the chemicals in your eyes, flush them with water for 10 minutes and then have a health care provider examine you.

Procedure

Experiment 1

1. Obtain three 13- x 100-mm or three 15- x 150-mm test tubes. Label them A, B, and C.

2. Add 5 drops of NaSal (sodium salicylate) solution to each test tube.

3. Add: 2 drops of $Fe(NO_3)_3$ solution to tube A; 4 drops to tube B; and 6 drops to tube C.

4. Add 5 mL of distilled water to each test tube and gently tap or shake the tube to mix the contents thoroughly.

5. Record your answers to the questions in the Observations and Results Table on the Worksheet.

6. Set tubes A, B, and C aside in a rack or a beaker.

Experiment 2
1. Obtain three 13- x 100-mm or three 15- x 150-mm test tubes. Label these D, E, and F.

2. Add 3 drops of $Fe(NO_3)_3$ solution to each test tube.

3. Add: 2 drops of NaSal solution to tube D;   4 drops to tube E;   and 6 drops to tube F.

4. Add 5 mL of distilled water to each test tube, and gently shake the tube to mix the contents well.

5. Record your answers to the questions in the Observations and Results Table on the Worksheet.

6. Set tubes D, E, and F aside in a rack or a beaker.

Experiment 3
1. Take one of the tubes (A–F) that is deeply colored and add to it 2 drops of 5% HCl (dilute hydrochloric acid).

2. Gently shake the test tube to mix the contents thoroughly.

3. Record your observation in the Observations and Results Table on the Worksheet.

Experiment 4
1. Select one of the tubes (A–F) that is deeply colored (but not the one used in Experiment 3).

2. Add 2 drops 5% of aqueous Na_3PO_4 (sodium phosphate) to the solution, and gently shake the test tube to mix the contents well.

3. Record what you see in the Observations and Results Table on the Worksheet.

Cleaning up
  Empty your test tubes (A–F) into the container provided by your instructor. The tubes can then be cleaned with soap and water.

Pre-Lab Exercise A
Describe the purpose of the experiment in a few complete sentences of your own phrasing.

Pre-Lab Exercise B
Make a list of the chemicals and equipment you need for this experiment.

Pre-Lab Exercise C

Hydrogen gas burns in oxygen to make water only, which is one reason why H_2 has been promoted as the fuel of the future. Hydrogen gas can be obtained by electrolysis of water—passing an electric current through an aqueous solution of ions. Explain why burning hydrogen to make water and decomposing water by electrolysis does not represent a reversible process.

Pre-Lab Exercise D

Batteries produce electricity by a chemical reaction. Some batteries can be recharged by passing an electric current through them, while many other batteries are not rechargeable. What does this suggest about the chemical reactions used in rechargeable versus non-rechargeable batteries?

Pre-Lab Exercise E

Look back at the table of data for the hypothetical reaction $A + B \rightleftharpoons Y + Z$ given in the introduction. Suggest how you could determine more precisely when the reaction reaches equilibrium.

Pre-Lab Exercise F

Look back at the table of data for the hypothetical reaction $A + B \rightleftharpoons Y + Z$. After 8 hours from the start of the experiment, would the reaction be at equilibrium, shift to the right, or shift to the left if you:

    a) added Z to the mixture? Explain briefly.

    b) added A to the mixture? Explain briefly.

    c) removed Y from the mixture? Explain briefly.

    d) removed B from the mixture? Explain briefly.

Pre-Lab Exercise G

Suppose that the reaction $A + B \rightleftharpoons Y + Z$ occurs in a liquid solution. Now imagine that product Z is not very soluble in the liquid and begins to crystallize or precipitate as it forms. Will that cause the reaction to shift to the left or to the right? Why?

Lab Worksheet   **Name:** _____   **Section:** _____

1. Complete the Observations and Results Table below.

Experiment 1	Color of Reaction Mixture	Intensity of Color [†]
Tube A		
Tube B		
Tube C		

Experiment 2	Color of Reaction Mixture	Intensity of Color [†]
Tube D		
Tube E		
Tube F		

Experiment 3	Initial Intensity of Color	Intensity after Adding HCl
Tube Used =		

Experiment 4	Initial Intensity of Color	Intensity after Adding Na_3PO_4
Tube Used =		

[†] In Experiments 1 & 2, simply indicate which tube of the three is darkest and which is least dark in color.
In Experiments 3 & 4, indicate whether the intensity of the color remains the same, becomes darker, or becomes fainter after adding the HCl or Na_3PO_4.

2. Write the equation for the reaction that occurs between the iron and salicylate ions.

3. What ion in the reaction equation you wrote in question 2 is colored? Is it a product or a reactant?

4. What does the intensity of color in the reaction tube indicate?

5. Notice that the amount of salicylate ion and the total volume of solution is the same for tubes A, B, and C in Experiment 1. What trend is apparent as the relative amount of iron ion in each solution changes?

6. Notice that the amount of iron ion and total volume of solution is the same for tubes D, E, and F in Experiment 2. What trend is apparent as the relative amount of salicylate ion in each solution changes?

7. Do the results of Experiments 1 and 2 by themselves prove that the reaction of iron and salicylate ions is reversible? Explain why or why not.

8. When hydrochloric acid is added to salicylate ion in water, the following reaction occurs:

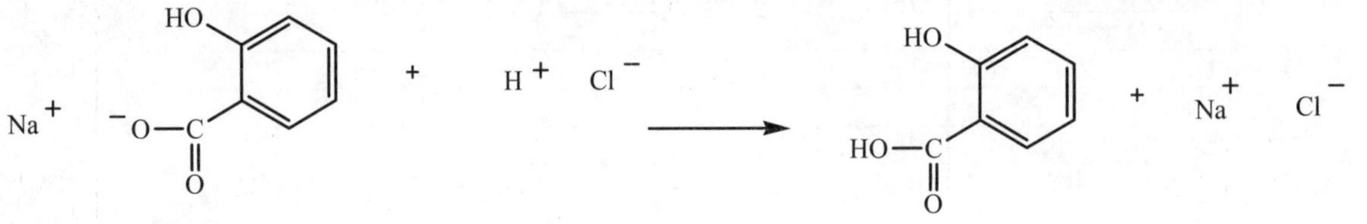

sodium salicylate	hydrochloric acid	salicylic acid	NaCl
$NaC_7H_5O_3$	HCl	$C_7H_6O_3$	sodium chloride

Salicylic acid is only slightly soluble in acidic water. Use this information to explain what you observed in Experiment 3.

9. Phosphate ion (PO_4^{-3}) and iron ion (Fe^{+3}) react to make the water-insoluble compound $FePO_4$. How does this help explain your observations for Experiment 4?

10. How do the results from Experiments 3 and 4 demonstrate that the reaction of Fe^{+3} and Sal^- (salicylate, $C_7H_6O_3^-$) is reversible?

11. Suppose that the product $[FeSal]^{+2}$ was not very soluble in water. Would this tend to make the reaction move more to the left or right? In other words, would it cause the reaction to produce more or less $[FeSal]^{+2}$ than in your experiment where the product is soluble?

Introduction

Water is truly an unusual compound. It is a liquid at temperatures where other low molecular-mass substances are gases. Water requires more heat to vaporize and freezes at a higher temperature than most small molecules. Unlike most solids, ice is less dense than liquid water, so it floats.

Stranger yet, water reacts by itself—ever so slightly but measurably—to dissociate into H^+ and OH^- ions (proton and hydroxide ions, respectively). This autoionization (self ionization) is reversible and can be written $H_2O \leftrightarrows H^+ + OH^-$. In almost no time at all, the forward and backwards reactions occur at the same speed, achieving equilibrium. Please remember that once a reversible reaction reaches equilibrium the concentrations of the reactants and products no longer change over time. When the autoionization reaction reaches equilibrium near room temperature, a liter of water contains about 56 moles H_2O, but only 1.00×10^{-7} moles H^+ and an equal number moles OH^-. Thus, the autoionization of H_2O does not occur to a significant extent.

The small concentrations of H^+ participating in the autoionization equilibrium can be expressed in scientific notation (e.g., 1.00×10^{-7}) or in a more compact way called "pH" where $pH = -\log[H^+]$. This expression means that the pH of a solution is calculated as the negative logarithm of the molarity of H^+. Please recall from lecture that molarity equals the moles of a substance found in one liter of solution. Since pure water at 25° C has a concentration of $H^+ = 1.0 \times 10^{-7}$ moles/Liter, the pH = 7.00; the concentration of OH^- in pure water at 25° C is also 1.0×10^{-7} moles/Liter. In direct analogy to pH the concentration of OH^- can be described as $pOH = -\log[OH^-]$. The concentrations of H^+ and OH^- are related through the autoionization equilibrium, and so pH and pOH are connected as well. In the same solution $pH + pOH = 14.00$, though we will not examine why this is true.

Scientists have long used the *pH scale* to describe the concentration of H^+ in an aqueous solution. The values of pH vary between 0 and 14, and fall into three ranges: acidic, neutral, and basic. A change in one pH unit represents a 10-fold change in concentration of H^+, while a difference of two pH units corresponds to a 100-fold change of H^+ concentration.

The pH Scale

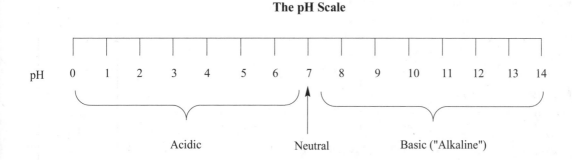

At 25° C *acidic solutions* have a concentration of H^+ greater than 1.00×10^{-7} moles/Liter, corresponding to a pH between 0 and 6.9; acidic solutions also contain more H^+ than OH^- ions. *Neutral solutions* have exactly equal concentrations of H^+ and OH^- (pH 7.00 at room temperature). *Basic* or *alkaline* solutions contain more hydroxide ion than hydrogen ion, so the concentration of H^+ is less than 1.00×10^{-7} moles/Liter, corresponding to a pH between 7 and 14.

Pure water is neutral (contains equals concentrations of hydroxide and hydrogen ions), but substances dissolved in water may upset the balance between H^+ and OH^- ions in solution.

Acids are substances that increase the concentration of H^+ in water. Because the autoionization of water is reversible *acids also cause a decrease in the amount of OH^- in the solution*. Increasing the number of moles of H^+ in the solution forces some OH^- ions to react and make more H_2O molecules. Another common definition of an acid is "a substance that releases H^+." Any compound that ionizes in water to produce H^+ and an anion also increases the concentration of H^+ in solution and thus is an acid.

Similarly, *bases are substances that increase the concentration of OH^- in water*, and consequently they *decrease the concentration of H^+ present*. Once again, the concentrations of OH^- and H^+ are inversely related because the autoionization of water is a reversible reaction. Bases are also described as "substances that release OH^- or react with H^+."

Acids and bases are present in the food and beverages we consume; they are formed as products of reactions in our cells; and many medications people take are acids or bases. It is not too surprising that scientists are interested in detecting the presence of an acid or base in a solution and want to know the concentration of H^+ or OH^-. As it so often happens, Nature itself provides the clues and tools to assist in this task.

Over the thousands of years that humans have cultivated plants, farmers and gardeners alike have noticed that the color of the flowers of some species of plants varies with the amount of acid or base in the soil. Chemists later discovered how to make pigments with similar behavior. Substances that change color in response to the concentration of H^+ in a solution are commonly called *acid-base indicators*.

Compounds that are acid-base indicators share several common characteristics:
- they contain conjugated systems of double bonds (see Waldron Chapters 3.4 and 5.7);
- they react reversibly with H^+ or OH^-; and
- the product of a reaction with H^+ or OH^- has a different color than the indicator.

Let's examine several examples of acid-base indicators to see why these characteristics are significant.

The compound known as "butter yellow" (a dye once used to artificially color butter) is also an acid-base indicator.

Notice that the molecule contains a set of conjugated C=C and N=N bonds. Delocalization of the electrons lowers the energy of the molecule enough that it absorbs light in the visible portion of the electromagnetic spectrum. Like the hydroxide ion (OH^-), the nitrogen atom in ammonia (NH_3) and related organic compounds called amines possesses an extra pair of electrons that can be shared with H^+ to make a bond. When an acid releases H^+ in the presence of butter yellow, one of the nitrogen atoms uses its unshared electron pair to make a bond with the hydrogen ion. The cation formed from the dye has both a different energy and color.

Butter yellow and its cation (red)

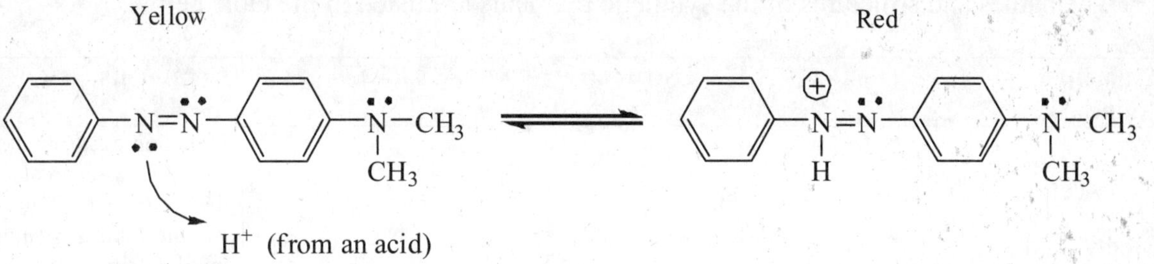

H$^+$ (from an acid)

As a second example, let's examine "phenolphthalein"—an indicator you may have used in junior or senior high school labs. Phenolphthalein (structure below at left) contains fewer C=C groups conjugated with each other than butter yellow; it is a white powder that gives a colorless solution in water. Hydroxide added to a solution of phenolphthalein removes an H$^+$ from a phenol group (the OH connected to the benzene ring) creating a more extensively conjugated pink-colored anion.

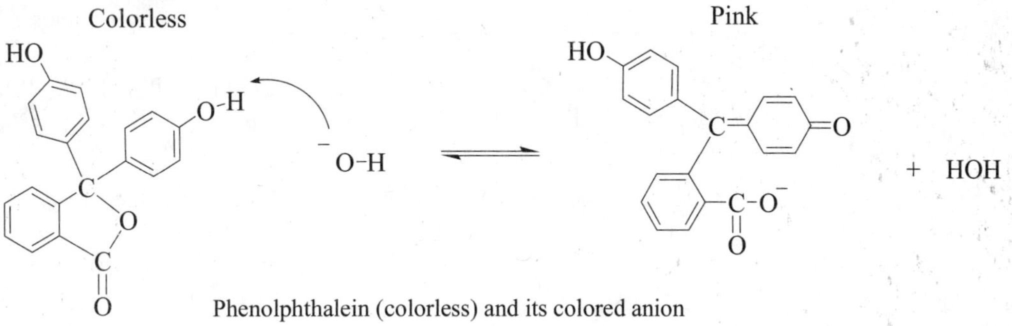

Phenolphthalein (colorless) and its colored anion

The chemical structure of an indicator determines the exact pH at which it changes color and what that color happens to be. For example, butter yellow is yellow in solutions having a pH 4 or higher, but red at pH 2.9 or less. Over the *transition range* (pH 2.9–4) a solution of butter yellow appears orange because both the red and yellow forms of the indicator are present in comparable concentrations. On the other hand, phenolphthalein is colorless in solutions that have a pH less than 8.00, but red above pH 10. In phenolphthalein's transition range (pH 8–10) the indicator is a light pink.

Chemists use the change in color of an indicator to detect a change in the pH of a solution during a reaction. The particular color of the solution shows or *indicates* what concentration of H$^+$ is present. An indicator is most useful over its transition range because very small changes in H$^+$ concentration produce easily discerned differences in the shade of color seen. For this reason, chemists have assembled a large collection of indicators that have transition ranges spread across the entire pH scale.

Background

In this experiment you are going to work with both synthetic and natural pigments to study their behavior as acid-base indicators. The synthetic pigments will be provided to you as ready-to-use dilute solutions, but the natural pigments first must be isolated or extracted from a source material. If the pigment is an acid-base indicator, you will then determine its transition range. Finally, you will use your observations to determine the approximate pH of an unknown solution.

The names and structures of the synthetic pigments are listed in the table below.

Pigment Name	Structure	Comments
Methyl Red		The ionic grouping O=C-O⁻ Na⁺ makes the pigment water-soluble, but is not involved in any acid-base reaction that causes a color change.
Congo Red		The ionic grouping SO₃⁻ Na⁺ makes the pigment water-soluble, but is not involved in any acid-base reaction that causes a color change.
Phenol Red		The OH group on the benzene rings react with OH⁻ the same way as phenol-phthalein.
Alizarin Yellow GG		The ionic grouping O=C-O⁻ Na⁺ makes the pigment water-soluble, but is not involved in any acid-base reaction that causes a color change.

The *anthocyanins* are a complex class of plant pigments that are acid-base indicators. Although these substances contain conjugated double bonds, they have a structure altogether different from those of the synthetic indicators just described.

General structure of an anthocyanin and its reaction with base

(X and Y can be H, OH, and/or OCH₃)

Anthocyanin   Product from reaction with base

Each specific anthocyanin has a different type of sugar, X, and Y group. The sugar (carbohydrate) portion of the anthocyanin makes the substance water soluble, while the particular color the pigment shows depends on whether X and/or Y are H, OH, or OCH_3 groups.

Notice that the oxygen atom in the center ring carries a positive charge: This is because it loans one of its normally unshared pairs of electrons to the adjacent ring carbon. When OH^- is present in solution it gives a pair of electrons to the ring carbon, allowing the oxygen atom to have its usual bonding arrangement of two single bonds and two unshared pairs. The color of changes because the number of conjugated double bonds is no longer the same.

The relationship between the structure of a compound, its color, and acid-base properties is much more complex than we have been able to describe in these few paragraphs, so please do not feel that you are missing something if you still have questions about the subject. A lot of the story has been left out in this short introduction!

Working Safely

The synthetic indicators are also dyes that may temporarily stain your skin if you spill some of the solution on yourself. (The stains will wash or wear off in a day or two.) Wear gloves if they are available.

Acid and base solutions are potential skin irritants, which is another reason for using gloves. If you spill some acid or base solution on your skin, immediately flush the chemical off with cold tap water. Because you will be using very small volumes of acids and base dispensed from dropper bottles, you should not expect to come into contact with significantly hazardous amounts of the reagents.

Most important, wear proper eye protection: safety glasses or goggles. Keep gloved and ungloved fingers out of your eyes, nose, mouth, and ears. If you do get some acid or base solution in your eyes, immediately flush them for several minutes at the eyewash fountain. Then consult with your instructor to determine if a visit to the campus health service is needed.

Isopropyl rubbing alcohol is flammable; there should be no open flames used in lab. Do not ingest this alcohol! Use the rubbing alcohol in a well-ventilated room or in the fume hood. Place waste alcohol in the waste container provided.

If you work with a partner you can easily examine the four synthetic indicators and two or more of the natural indicators.

Procedure for testing synthetic indicators

Your instructor will provide a series of aqueous (water) solutions at about pH 1 to 12 in small dispensing bottles. In this experiment it is not necessary to know what particular acid or base is in the solution—only the pH is relevant.

The synthetic indicators are dilute solutions in water as well. It is important to note on the label which indicator you are using. For simplicity these abbreviations may be used:

MR = Methyl Red
CR = Congo Red
PR = Phenol Red
AY = Alizarin Yellow GG

Acid-Base Indicators

1. Obtain a glass or plastic well plate that accommodates at least 12 samples. If you are using a clear plastic plate, place a sheet of plain white paper under it to make it easier to see the color contrasts between the different samples.

2. Place 1 drop of the *same* indicator solution in each of the 12 wells of the plate.

3. Add about 10 drops (approximately 0.5 mL) of a solution of known, but different, pH to each well. For example, add pH 1 solution to well 1; pH 2 solution to well 2, and so on. Use a consistent pattern for adding the solutions to each well. (You could make a simple grid showing which well has which pH solution in it.)

4. If the color of a solution in an individual well is not uniform mix the liquid with a small glass rod. Rinse the rod with water between samples.

5. Record the color of each solution in Data Table 1 on the Worksheet.

6. Rinse out the wells at the sink with tap water and once with deionized or distilled water. Dry the plate wells with paper.

7. Repeat steps 1-6 for each synthetic indicator solution you plan to test.

Procedure for testing the natural indicators

Purple *Concord grape* juice and red *cranberry juice* are available at most grocery stores and can be used as bought.

Enough *red cabbage* juice for a lab section is made by chopping about ½ of a small head of red cabbage with water in a blender and filtering off the solids. On a smaller scale, several pieces of cabbage leaf may be cut up and ground in a mortar with enough water to cover the leaves; the liquid can be decanted or filtered away from the vegetable residue. (Note: Some people do not like the smell of cabbage!)

Hibiscus leaves are found in some non-caffeinated herbal teas. For example, Celestial Seasonings® makes several types of teas called Zingers™ which include dried hibiscus (e.g., Raspberry Zinger and Red Zinger). Steep one of these tea bags in 50 mL of hot water until the liquid cools to room temperature. Squeeze the excess tea from the bag with a spoon and discard it before using the tea as an indicator.

Any number of flowers, fruits, or vegetables contain pigments that could be tested for indicator activity. Depending on seasonal availability you might try red radish skins; blueberries or service berries; or petals of hollyhocks, delphiniums, petunias, hydrangea, or others of your choice. Tear or cut up the plant tissue into small pieces, place them in a small beaker, and add enough rubbing alcohol to cover the solids. Usually grinding the plant matter as you stir it with a glass rod will extract the colored pigments. The solution should have a noticeably dark color to it before you can use it as an indicator.

Turmeric is a common kitchen condiment sold in the spice section of the grocery store. Place about 250 mg of turmeric in a 13- x 100-mm test tube. Add enough isopropyl rubbing alcohol (70% 2-propanol in water) to half-fill the tube. Use a glass stirring rod to mix the solid with the alcohol. Let the solids settle to the bottom of the tube and use the liquid as the indicator. *The extract can be tested using the same procedure as for the synthetic dyes.*

The juices and extracts from the other plant materials are more dilute than the synthetic dyes and should be tested as follows:

1. Label twelve 12- x 75-mm test tubes 1–12 to correspond to the pH of the solution to be added.

2. Measure with a plastic transfer pipette 1 mL of the same juice or plant extract into each tube.

3. Add 5–10 drops of a solution of known pH to each test tube, so that pH 1 solution is added to the tube labeled #1, pH 2 solution is added to tube #2, and so on.

4. Gently agitate each tube until the solution has a uniform color.

5. Record the color of each solution in Data Table 2 on the Worksheet.

6. Follow your instructor's directions for disposal of the test solutions.

7. Rinse out the tubes with water before using them to test another indicator.

8. Repeat steps 1–7. For each indicator you plan to test.

Estimating the pH of an unknown

Obtain a sample solution from your instructor. The objective is to test the sample with the minimum number of indicators to estimate the pH of the unknown based on the data you collected in this experiment. [**Hint**: First consider what natural or synthetic indicator you might use to determine if the unknown has a pH less than or greater than 7. Then consider which indicators would help you narrow down the possible range of pH values.] Finally, report that the solution has a pH between __ and __.

Record your observations in Data Table 3 on the Worksheet.

Pre-Lab Exercise A

Describe the purpose of the experiment in a few complete sentences of your own phrasing.

Pre-Lab Exercise B

Make a list of the chemicals and equipment you need for this experiment.

Pre-Lab Exercise C

Indicators like butter yellow which react with H^+ are called *basic indicators*. Explain why butter yellow is a base.

Pre-Lab Exercise D

Indicators like phenolphthalein which react with OH^- are called *acidic indicators*. Explain why phenolphthalein is an acid.

Acid-Base Indicators

Pre-Lab Exercise E

Classify each of the following indicators as an acidic or basic indicator, and briefly justify your answer. The structures for the indicators were given earlier.

a) Methyl Red

c) Phenol Red

b) Congo Red

d) Alizarin Yellow GG

Pre-Lab Exercise F

The structure of the anion obtained when phenolphthalein reacts with OH^- is given below. Highlight or draw a loop around the atoms that are involved in the conjugated double bonds (see Waldron Chapters 3.4 and 5.7).

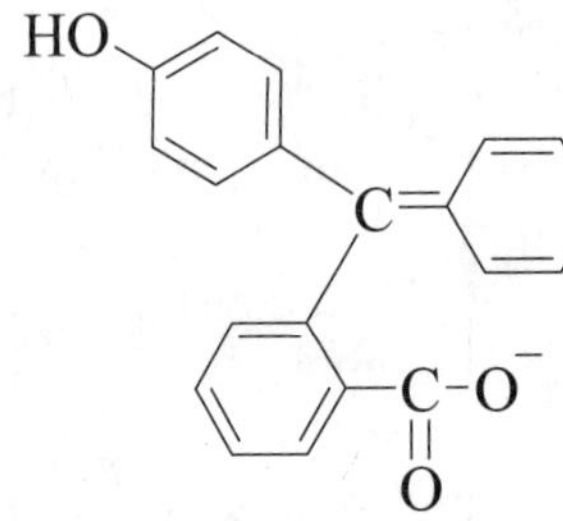

Pre-Lab Exercise G

The substance in turmeric which is an indicator is called *curcumin*:

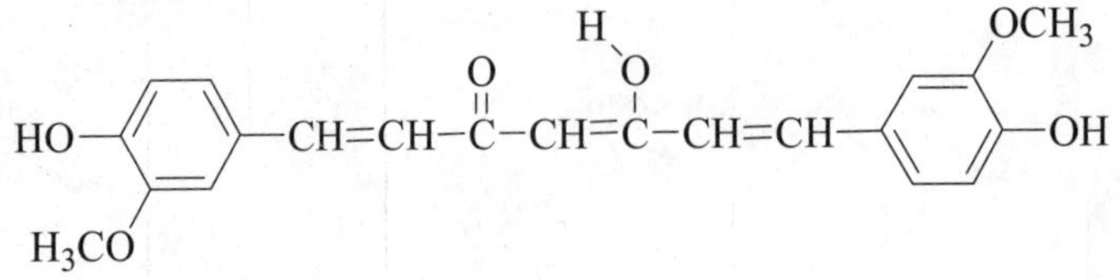

a) Curcumin is an acidic indicator. Identify which H might be released as H^+ when curcumin reacts with OH^-.

b) Identify the atoms which make up the conjugated system in curcumin.

Pre-Lab Exercise H

Look back at the general structure of an anthocyanin and its product formed by reaction with OH^-. Which substance contains more conjugated bonds?

Lab Worksheet   Name: _____   Section: _____

1. Complete Data Table 1 for the observations of tests made with the synthetic indicators in solutions at different pH values:

pH of Solution Tested	Color Seen with Methyl Red (MR)	Color Seen with Congo Red (CR)	Color Seen with Phenol Red (PR)	Color Seen with Alizarin Yellow GG (AY)
1				
2				
3				
4				
5				
6				
7				
8				
9				
10				
11				
12				

2. Use your observations in Data Table 1 to determine the transition pH range for each indicator and its transition color; the indicator's color at pH lower (or more acidic) than the transition range;   and its color at a pH higher (or less acidic) than the transition range.   Report your findings in Results Table 1:

Indicator	Transition pH range	Transition Color	Color at lower pH	Color at Higher pH
Methyl Red (MR)				
Congo Red (CR)				
Phenol Red (PR)				
Alizarin Yellow (AY)				

3. Complete Data Table 2 for the observations of tests made with the four natural indicators in solutions at different pH values:

pH of Solution	Color Seen with 1. (name)	Color Seen with 2. (name)	Color Seen with 3. (name)	Color Seen with 4. (name)
1				
2				
3				
4				
5				
6				
7				
8				
9				
10				
11				
12				

5. Based on the observations you recorded in Data Table 2 what is the:
   a) transition pH range for each indicator?
   b) transition color of the indicator?
   c) color of the indicator at pH lower (or more acidic) than the transition range?
   d) color of the indicator at a pH higher (or less acidic) than the transition range?

   Report your findings in Results Table 2:

Indicator	Transition pH range	Transition Color	Color at lower pH	Color at Higher pH
1)				
2)				
3)				
4)				

6. Do any of the natural indicators appear to have more than one transition range? That is, are there two narrow regions of pH that have distinct color? What are they?

7. Record your observations from testing the unknown in Data Table 3:

Indicator Used to Test Unknown	Color Observed	Inference

8. Why should you report the pH of your unknown as a range (e.g., pH 3–4)?

   Based on your observations in Data Table 3, what appears to be the pH of your unknown? Explain briefly.

9. Why is this method of estimating the pH of a sample not convenient or precise?

10. How many different indicators would you need to estimate precisely the acidity of a sample over a range of pH 1–12?

Companion Sections in Waldron: Chapters 4.4 and 4.6

Introduction

In the last experiment ("pH Pointers—Acid-Base Indicators") we saw that it is possible to determine whether a solution is acidic, basic, or neutral using pigments that change color in response to the pH of the solution. Now let's see how it is possible to determine the quantity of acid or base in a sample.

An *acid* can be defined as "any substance that increases the concentration of H^+ in water." This can be expressed in the form of a chemical equation: $HA \rightarrow H^+ + A^-$. The symbol A^- represents the anion (negatively charged particle) that is left behind when the hydrogen ion (H^+) is released.

Although the concentration of H^+ in a solution determines the pH of the mixture, the structure of HA determines how easily and how many moles of H^+ are released from each mole of HA. Not all H in a compound are acidic. Chemists have learned that in order for HA to lose H^+, the anion A^- must be of low energy in water. Generally, this means that the negative charge is associated with an electronegative element such as F, Cl, Br, I, or O (see Waldron Chapter 2.2). Thus, these compounds are acids: HF (hydrofluoric acid, used to etch glass); HCl (hydrochloric acid, found in the stomach); HBr (hydrobromic acid), and HI (hydriodic acid). Most other acids usually have the acidic H bonded to an oxygen atom in HA. Some examples are tabulated below.

Name	Formula	Structure	Condensed Structure	Comments
Sulfuric Acid	H_2SO_4	$HO-\overset{\overset{O}{\|\|}}{\underset{\underset{O}{\|\|}}{S}}-OH$	$(HO)_2SO_2$	Sulfuric acid is a *diprotic acid*: each mole of H_2SO_4 can release 2 moles of H^+.
Nitric Acid	HNO_3	structure	$HONO_2$	Nitric acid is a *monoprotic* acid: each mole of HNO_3 can release 1 mole of H^+.
Acetic Acid	$C_2H_4O_2$	$H-\overset{\overset{H}{\|}}{\underset{\underset{H}{\|}}{C}}-\overset{\overset{O}{\|\|}}{C}-OH$	CH_3CO_2H	Acetic acid is *monoprotic* – only the H attached to O in the CO_2H group is acidic.
Phosphoric Acid	H_3PO_4	$HO-\overset{\overset{O}{\|\|}}{\underset{\underset{OH}{\|}}{P}}-OH$	$(HO)_3PO$	Phosphoric acid is *triprotic*: 3 moles of H^+ can be released per mole of H_3PO_4.

Hydrochloric (and HF, HBr, and HI), sulfuric, nitric, and phosphoric acids are traditionally called *mineral acids*, since they do not contain carbon. Acetic acid (found in vinegar) contains carbon and hydrogen bonds: It is an organic acid called a *carboxylic acid*. Carboxylic acids are the most common organic acids and are easily recognized because their structure always contains the carboxyl group, $-CO_2H$ (sometimes written $-COOH$). The dash indicates the bond that connects the acid group to the rest of the molecule.

Bases are the other side of the coin. A *base* is "a substance that increases the concentration of hydroxide ion (OH^-) in water." Oven and drain cleaners often contain lye, which is the common name for sodium hydroxide, NaOH.

Bases also are "H^+ acceptors," which means the base donates an electron pair to H^+ to form a covalent bond. When the base is OH^- the product is water:

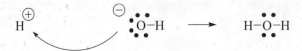

When an equal number of moles of an acid and base are mixed the acid-base reaction is called a *neutralization* and can be described by the equation

$$HA + NaOH \rightarrow H_2O + NaA.$$

NaA represents the ionic compound Na^+A^-. Long ago all ionic compounds were referred to as "salts." Thus, you may have heard a neutralization reaction explained as "the reaction of an acid and a base to make water and a salt." This definition is not satisfactory for describing all neutralization reactions because the base may not be hydroxide ion. Nonetheless, it does suggest a very practical way to determine the quantity of acid in a substance. Let's see how this might be accomplished.

For each mole of H^+ produced by an acid, the equation above tells us that one mole of OH^- is needed. The number of moles of H^+ could be determined by neutralizing it with a base if:

> (1) the completion of the neutralization reaction can be detected, and
> (2) the number of moles of OH^- used can be measured.

Both of these objectives are easy to satisfy.

Imagine that the acid HA is dissolved in some water along with a small quantity of an appropriate indicator. As long as the solution is acidic, the color of the indicator will remain unchanged. As base is added to the mixture, HA is gradually consumed until just enough OH^- has been added to completely neutralize the acid. The next tiniest amount of base added will make the pH of the solution larger than 7 (which is neutral). If the correct indicator has been chosen, an immediate color change will signal that the neutralization reaction is complete.

Now, how can we determine the number of moles of OH^- needed to exactly neutralize the acid? Like most ionic compounds, NaOH dissolves in water. Imagine that we have dissolved a known number of moles NaOH in each liter of solution. In other words, the molarity or molar concentration of the aqueous NaOH is known. All that is needed to complete the experiment is a precise way to deliver a measured volume of the NaOH solution into the sample of the acid and indicator. The device needed to do this was invented in the late 18th century; a *burette* is a long cylindrical glass tube with a valve at the bottom to control the volume and speed of the liquid drained from it. A scale marked along the length of the burette indicates the level of the liquid in the tube. If the liquid level is noted at the start and end of the neutralization reaction, the exact volume of base solution added is known. A sketch of the apparatus is shown in Figure 11-1.

Finally, an easy calculation gives the result of the experiment. Since Molarity = moles solute/Liter of solution, then

Molarity of NaOH x Liters of solution = moles of NaOH added.

Recall that one mole of H^+ reacts with one mole OH^-. Thus, the moles of NaOH added to neutralize the acid equals the number of moles of acid in the sample.

This method of using a burette to measure the volume of a solution of known concentration needed to completely react with a substance being analyzed is called a *titration*. The technique is not limited to neutralization reactions, but it is certainly one of the most common applications. For that reason, the method is often referred to as an "acid-base titration."

Background

A short walk down the "soft drink" aisle of any grocery store will quickly demonstrate the popularity of these beverages. There seem to be two major groups of drinks, the caramel-colored "colas" and the "non-colas." Most of the beverages contain carbonated water, a sweetener, preservatives, and a blend of flavoring agents. The non-colas typically include citric acid to provide citrus fruit-like "tartness" to the drink.

Citric acid is a naturally occurring substance that plays a prominent role in the breakdown of fats, proteins, and carbohydrates in the body (Waldron Chapter 12.5).

$$
\begin{array}{c}
\overset{\displaystyle O}{\underset{\displaystyle |}{\overset{\displaystyle \|}{C}}}OH \\
| \\
HOC-CH_2-C-CH_2-COH \qquad \text{Citric acid} \\
| \\
OH
\end{array}
$$

Although there are four oxygen atoms bonded to hydrogen in a molecule of citric acid, only three of these are in carboxylic acid groups; the fourth OH group is an "alcohol" which is non-acidic in water. Thus, citric acid is classified as a triprotic acid: One mole of this compound will require *three* moles of NaOH in a neutralization reaction. The reaction equation is $C_6H_8O_7$ (citric acid) $+ \; 3 \; NaOH \rightarrow 3 \; H_2O + Na_3C_6H_5O_7$ (sodium citrate).

This experiment concerns determining the citric acid content of Mountain Dew™ by titration with sodium hydroxide. This particular brand of beverage was chosen for its popularity, wide availability, and because it also is used in several other experiments in this text. You may want to try other brands of soft drinks, but make sure that the label lists citric acid near the top of the ingredient list before attempting the titration.

Citric acid is not the only source of H^+ in the beverage. Like other carbonated beverages, Mountain Dew gets its "pop" and some of its acid "bite" from the carbon dioxide dissolved under pressure in the water. If carbon dioxide (CO_2) has no hydrogens, how can it be an acid?

The traditional explanation is that CO_2 reacts with water to make H_2CO_3 (carbonic acid), or $CO_2 + H_2O \rightarrow H_2CO_3$. Carbonic acid then releases H^+ into the solution by partially dissociating:

$$
\underset{\text{carbonic acid}}{HO-\overset{\displaystyle O}{\overset{\displaystyle \|}{C}}-OH} \; \rightleftharpoons \; \underset{\text{bicarbonate ion}}{HO-\overset{\displaystyle O}{\overset{\displaystyle \|}{C}}-O^{\ominus}} \; + \; H^{\oplus}
$$

If you titrate the soft drink from a recently opened bottle or can, the NaOH will neutralize both citric acid and carbonic acid. This is why the instructions tell you to titrate *flat* Mountain Dew—most of the CO_2 will have escaped. Even so, a small amount of CO_2 remains dissolved and causes an overestimate of the amount of citric acid present (unless the solution is heated to drive off the carbon dioxide).

Knowing the molarity of the NaOH solution is important because the base is the reference point for determining how much citric acid is in the drink. Be sure to record the value from the supply bottle or blackboard!

It is easy to perform a sloppy and inaccurate titration. With only slightly more care and attention to detail, the analysis can be conducted carefully and precisely. Familiarize yourself with the set-up and use of the apparatus in Figures 11-1 and 11-2.

Even experienced chemists first perform a "practice" titration to obtain an approximation of the total volume of base needed to complete the neutralization. Several "good quality" titrations typically are used and the results averaged for the actual analysis of the acid in the sample. You should perform at least one practice and one "good" titration in your experiment.

The list of "Titration Tips" (following Figures 11-1 and 11-2) will provide some assistance in completing this experiment successfully.

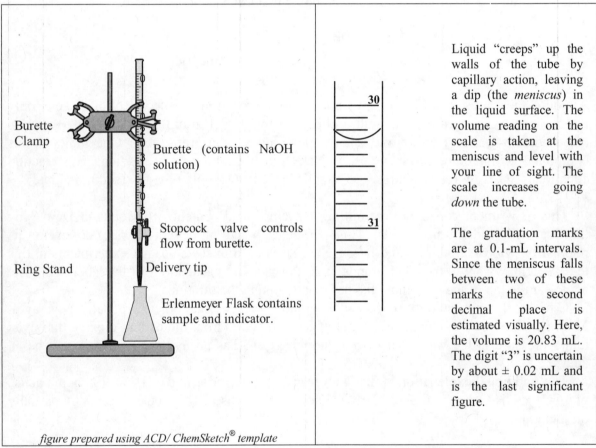

Burette Clamp

Burette (contains NaOH solution)

Stopcock valve controls flow from burette.

Ring Stand

Delivery tip

Erlenmeyer Flask contains sample and indicator.

figure prepared using ACD/ ChemSketch® template

Liquid "creeps" up the walls of the tube by capillary action, leaving a dip (the *meniscus*) in the liquid surface. The volume reading on the scale is taken at the meniscus and level with your line of sight. The scale increases going *down* the tube.

The graduation marks are at 0.1-mL intervals. Since the meniscus falls between two of these marks the second decimal place is estimated visually. Here, the volume is 20.83 mL. The digit "3" is uncertain by about ± 0.02 mL and is the last significant figure.

Figure 11-1: Apparatus for a titration   Figure 11-2: Reading a burette scale

Titration Tips

1. Before filling the burette make sure the stopcock valve is <u>closed</u> (i.e., handle is parallel to floor).

2. Use a funnel to add liquid to the burette.

3. Drain some liquid through the stopcock before the first titration to push out air bubbles in the

delivery tip (the glass tube projecting below the stopcock).

4. The liquid level should be near the top of the burette before a titration is started, but it does not need to be placed exactly at the 0.0 mark.   Record this reading as the starting volume.

5. Swirl the flask during the addition of reagent from the burette to enhance mixing, or use a magnetic stirrer.

6. Before deciding that the indicator has changed color, knock the drop of liquid from the burette delivery tip into the flask. You are looking for the first detectable change in color that persists for at least 30 seconds.   Record this as the final volume.

7. The net volume of reagent added equals the final volume minus the starting volume.

Working Safely
   Sodium hydroxide solution is caustic, which means it can cause a chemical burn if left in contact with the skin. Do wear disposable gloves if they are available, and keep your fingers out of your ears, nose, eyes, and mouth.
   You must wear eye protection at all times when NaOH solution is being used (by you or a nearby worker). If base is splashed in the eyes, immediately flush them at the eyewash fountain for at least 10 minutes. Someone should alert your instructor so that a health care professional can examine your eyes after they have been flushed.
   The mixture left in your Erlenmeyer flask at the conclusion of a titration may be flushed down the sink unless local regulations prohibit this practice. Any excess NaOH solution should be placed in the container provided by your instructor.

Procedure

1. Arrange the burette and other equipment as shown in Figure 11-1. Use a 250-mL Erlenmeyer flask for the titration.

2. Fill the burette with NaOH solution using a funnel. (*Wear goggles and gloves!*) Record the concentration (molarity) of the base in the Data Table on the Worksheet.

3. Measure out 100 mL of flat Mountain Dew in a graduated cylinder and transfer it to the 250-mL Erlenmeyer flask. (If you will be using a magnetic stirrer, place a stir bar in the flask as well.)

4. Add 2–3 drops of the phenolphthalein indicator solution to the soft drink. Since the indicator is colorless in acidic solution, the color of the liquid should not change.

5. Clear any air bubbles from the delivery tip by draining and discarding some NaOH solution.

6. Read the level of the NaOH solution in the burette at the meniscus, and record the starting volume in the Data Table.

7. Place the mouth of the Erlenmeyer flask under the delivery tip of the burette, with the tip just inside the mouth. (If you are using a magnetic stirrer, the flask sits atop the stirring motor.)

8. Swirl the flask by hand [or start the stirrer] as you drain NaOH solution from the burette. The total volume needed will be somewhere between 20 and 30 mL. When you begin to see a few

streaks of a different color appear in the flask, stop adding the base. Knock the drop of liquid on the delivery tip into the flask.

9. When the neutralization of the citric acid is complete, the first extra droplet of NaOH will cause phenolphthalein to change color. Because Mountain Dew contains a yellow dye the solution will become salmon colored (or pink grapefruit or peach-orange depending on how you perceive the color). The actual tone of the color is not important: The first change in color that persists for about 30 seconds means the titration is complete.

10. Read the level of NaOH in the burette and record the value as the final volume in the Data Table.

11. Discard the neutralization mixture in the 250-mL Erlenmeyer flask. (Recover the stir bar first if you used one—another magnetic stirring bar inserted into the end of a piece of plastic tubing makes this easy and keeps your fingers clean.) Rinse the flask with water to remove all traces of base.

12. Refill the burette with NaOH solution of the same concentration used for the last titration. Don't forget: use a funnel! and wear eye protection!

13. Repeat steps 1–11 for the next titration.

Pre-Lab Exercise A
Describe the purpose of the experiment in a few complete sentences of your own phrasing.

Pre-Lab Exercise B
Make a list of the chemicals and equipment you need for this experiment.

Pre-Lab Exercise C
If the molecular formula of citric acid is $C_6H_8O_7$, show how to calculate its molar mass (also called the molecular weight)?
Use these atomic weights: $C = 12.01$, $H = 1.01$, and $O = 16.00$
Hint: Review Waldron Chapter 2.4

Pre-Lab Exercise D
On the structure at the right, draw a circle around each of the hydrogen atoms in citric acid that can be released as H^+ in water.

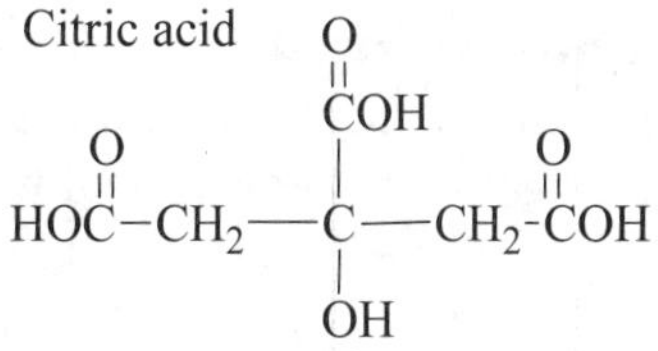

Imagine that you had an aqueous solution containing 0.025 moles of citric acid. How many moles of NaOH would be required to completely neutralize the acid?

Citric acid

$$\begin{array}{c} O \\ \| \\ \text{COH} \end{array}$$

$$\text{HOC}-\text{CH}_2-\underset{\underset{\text{OH}}{|}}{\overset{\overset{O}{\|}}{\underset{|}{C}}}-\text{CH}_2\text{-COH}$$

Pre-Lab Exercise E
Is carbonic acid (H_2CO_3) a monoprotic, diprotic, or triprotic acid? Explain.

Pre-Lab Exercise F

The two figures at the right show the liquid level in a burette at the start and finish of a titration. The scale is graduated in 0.1-mL increments.

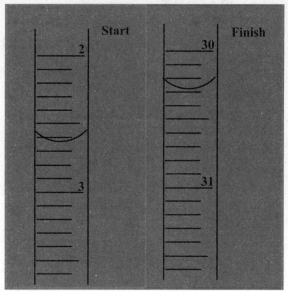

What was the net total volume of liquid dispensed?

What was the net volume in liters?

If the burette contained 0.12 M NaOH, how many moles of NaOH were collected?

Pre-Lab Exercise G

An aqueous solution of citric acid needed 0.36 moles of NaOH for complete neutralization. How many moles of citric acid were in the solution?

Pre-Lab Exercise H

A sample of a soft drink was titrated and needed 0.12 moles of NaOH for complete neutralization. How many grams of citric acid were contained in the beverage sample?

Lab Worksheet   **Name:** _____   **Section:** _____

1. Complete the Data Table below for each of your titrations.

	Practice Titration	Titration #1	Titration #2	Titration #3
Molarity of NaOH used				
Starting Volume (mL)				
Final Volume (mL)				
Net Volume of NaOH (mL)				
Net Volume of NaOH (L)				

2. Using the data for Titration #1, show how to calculate the:
a) moles of NaOH needed to neutralize the citric acid in the 100-mL sample of Mountain Dew.

b) moles of citric acid in the 100-mL sample of Mountain Dew.

c) grams of citric acid contained in 100-mL of Mountain Dew.

3. A 12-ounce can of Mountain Dew contains approximately 355 mL. Based on your calculations in question 2, how many grams of citric acid are ingested by drinking one can of Mountain Dew ?

4. If you performed more titrations, what is the average mass of citric acid found in 100 mL of Mountain Dew? (Or, you could list the results from several other students.)

5. Look back at step 9 of the procedure. Why do we use a faint but persistent change in the color of the solution to mark the completion of the neutralization reaction? Why is it wrong to add NaOH until the reaction acquires a deep and intense color?

6. Imagine that the following experiments were performed:

   Experiment #1   A 100-mL portion of Mountain Dew from a freshly opened bottle was titrated with NaOH.

   Experiment #2   The soft drink remaining in the bottle was stirred overnight in an open beaker. Then a 100-mL portion of the "flat" drink was titrated with NaOH.

   Experiment #3   The leftover "flat" soft drink was heated without evaporating any water. After the beverage was cooled to room temperature a 100-mL sample was titrated with NaOH.

   a) Will the volume of NaOH needed to titrate a 100-mL sample of Mountain Dew be the same for each of the experiments? Why or why not?

   b) What could be deduced by comparing the results of Experiments #2 and #3 ? (no calculations needed)

   c) What could be deduced by comparing the results of Experiments #1 and #3 ? (no calculations needed)

12   Some Light Work
- An Introduction to Spectroscopy -

Companion Section in Waldron: Chapter 5.7

Introduction

"Light" is called "electromagnetic radiation" by scientists; it is a form of energy traveling in waves made up of both electric and magnetic components. Electromagnetic radiation can travel through both matter and empty space.

Electromagnetic radiation is described in terms of its *speed* of travel, *wavelength*, and *frequency*. The velocity, or speed, is the distance the wave travels in a unit of time, just as the speed of a car is measured in miles per hour. Electromagnetic radiation travels most rapidly through a vacuum and more slowly through matter. For example, the speed of light is about 3×10^8 meters/second in a vacuum and is only slightly slower in air, but is 2.3×10^8 meters/second in water (1/4 slower than in a vacuum) and is 2×10^8 meters/second in glass (1/3 slower than in a vacuum).

The wavelength is the distance between successive peaks or dips in the wave curve (Figure 12-1), while the frequency is the number of peaks in the wave that pass by a fixed point in space each second. Wavelength (λ), frequency (ν), and speed of light (c) are related as

$$\text{speed} = \text{frequency} \times \text{wavelength or } c = \nu \cdot \lambda.$$

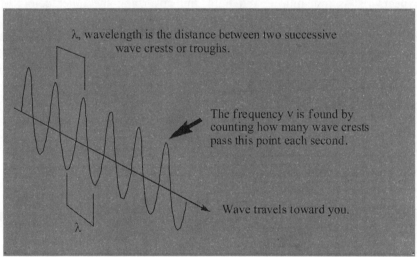

Figure 12-1: Terms describing electromagnetic radiation

The *electromagnetic spectrum* arranges the different types of electromagnetic radiation in order of their frequency or wavelength, and each region of the spectrum has a name as well. The energy of a particular type of light increases with its frequency.

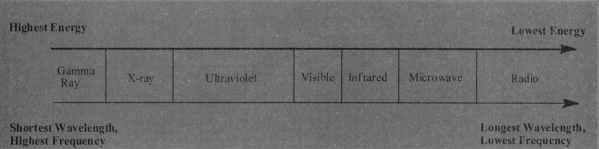

Figure 12-2: The electromagnetic spectrum

In everyday language "light" is the visible portion of the electromagnetic spectrum—a mixture of red, orange, yellow, green, blue, and violet light.

Color of Light	Wavelength in nm (1 nanometer = 1 x 10^{-9} m)
Red	720–620
Orange	620–580
Yellow	580–530
Green	530–480
Blue	480–420
Violet	400–420

Visible light makes up a very small band of the total electromagnetic spectrum, but it is important to humans because our eyes are sensitive to these wavelengths.

When we look at an object illuminated by natural or artificial white light, our eyes are responding to the wavelengths that are being reflected off the object or transmitted through it. If an object appears white to our eyes, it is reflecting all the colors of visible light. On the other hand, a black object is absorbing all the colors of visible light.

As a beam of electromagnetic radiation passes through a chemical sample, some frequencies of light are absorbed by the sample, while others are transmitted (passed through) unchanged. Thus, a solution that appears red is transmitting red light, but absorbing the other colors of the spectrum (mostly green and blue).

The absorbed light energy is transferred to a chemical substance and "excites" it; electrons are raised to higher energy orbitals by ultraviolet and visible light. Other types of electromagnetic radiation excite matter differently. For example, infrared light causes covalent bonds to stretch, twist, and bend.

A spectrophotometer (Figure 12-3) is an instrument consisting of a source of light for one part of the spectrum (e.g., a light bulb for white light); a means for selecting a narrow range of wavelengths of light to be used in the experiment (such as a prism or diffraction grating); a transparent container to hold the sample; a photoelectric eye that measures the amount of light striking it; and a meter, scale, or computer connection that reports the amount of light striking the photoelectric eye.

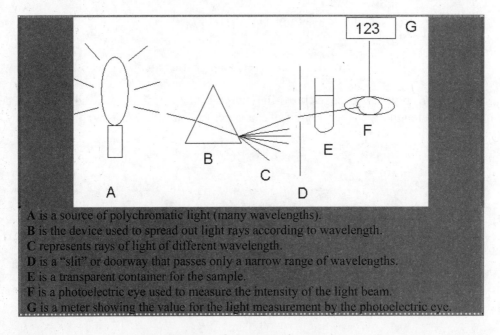

A is a source of polychromatic light (many wavelengths).
B is the device used to spread out light rays according to wavelength.
C represents rays of light of different wavelength.
D is a "slit" or doorway that passes only a narrow range of wavelengths.
E is a transparent container for the sample.
F is a photoelectric eye used to measure the intensity of the light beam.
G is a meter showing the value for the light measurement by the photoelectric eye.

Figure 12-3: Schematic diagram of a spectrophotometer

Spectrophotometers are basic instruments used for everyday work in medical, biological, chemical, and forensic laboratories to determine:
- what wavelengths of light a sample absorbs, and
- how much light a sample absorbs at a particular wavelength.

In this experiment you will use a spectrophotometer with a visible light source to determine the absorption spectrum of a food dye and determine the relationship between the concentration of dye in a solution and the amount of light absorbed.

Background

A spectrophotometer will provide two kinds of information about the power of the light after it passes through a sample. The *transmittance* (T) of a solution is defined as the ratio of the light power after it passes through a sample (P) compared to the power of the light before it enters the sample (P_0).

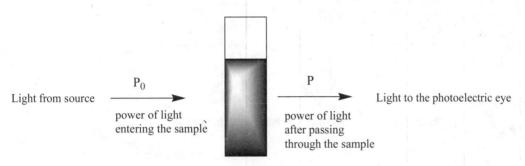

$$\text{Transmittance} = P/P_0$$

Since transmittance is a ratio or fraction, the number value ranges between 0 and 1. It is common practice to report the percent transmittance (%T) of a solution. This is simply the values of the transmittance multiplied by 100%.

Spectrophotometers also report the interaction of light with a sample in *absorbance* units. The absorbance of a sample equals the negative logarithm of the sample's transmittance; that is,

$$\text{Absorbance} = -\log(\text{Transmittance}), \text{ or } A = -\log(T).$$

To calculate the absorbance of a solution from its percentage transmittance, the %T value must be divided by 100 before the logarithm is taken: $\text{Absorbance} = -\log(\%T/100)$.

One type of spectrophotometer widely used in instructional laboratories is known as the *Spectronic 20®* (sometimes referred to as the "Spec20"). Over the past 40 years several different manufacturers have produced one model or the other of this instrument. More recently other spectroscopic instruments interfaced to a computer, graphing calculator, or other hand-held device have become common as well. Figure 12-4 briefly describes the *Spectronic 20*-type of instrument and how it is used. Since your lab may have a different instrument, please be especially attentive to your instructor's directions for its correct use.

On an analog spectrophotometer the transmittance and absorbance readings are indicated by a needle pointing at numbers on a scale. The %T values are much easier to read because the scale is linear and the spacing between marks is constant, making it possible to estimate the last significant digit. By contrast, it is much more difficult to read absorbance values on an analog scale since the spacing between marks is logarithmic. Of course, if you have an instrument with a digital meter the problem disappears!

We will be using both %T and absorbance readings in this experiment. If your spectrophotometer has a digital readout, simply record both values. In case you have an analog meter, read and record the %T values only—it is much easier to calculate the absorbance from these later.

Obtaining a *spectrum* of a chemical sample is usually the first step in a spectroscopic analysis. The spectrum is a graph that plots how the transmittance or absorbance of a sample changes with the wavelength of light used to excite the compounds in the sample. The wavelength(s) at which the sample absorbs light most (or transmits the least light) provides information about the type of chemical in the sample. Similarly, this wavelength is especially useful for monitoring how the transmittance or absorbance of the solution changes with changes in the concentration of the sample.

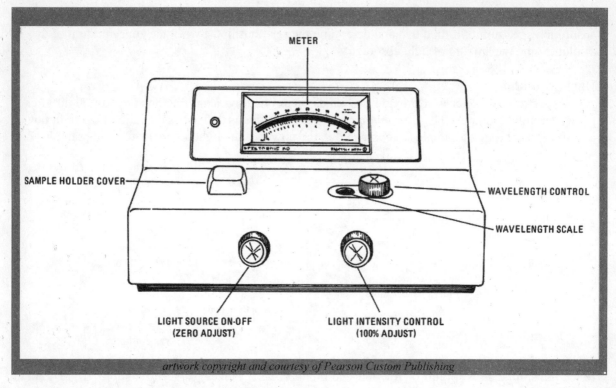

Figure 12-4: The *Spectronic 20* spectrophotometer.
(a) The on/off knob is also used to set the 0% T (called the "dark current") when no tube is in the sample compartment.
(b) The 100% T must be reset every time the wavelength of the light beam is changed. Place a tube of distilled water in the sample compartment and adjust the front right dial to read 100%.
(c) If your instrument has a needle and analog meter, read the %T value on the scale from the angle at which you can not see the needle's reflection in the mirror. If your instrument has a digital readout, check that the mode button is set to transmittance or absorbance before recording the number value.

Procedure
Determining the Visible Spectrum of a Food Dye

1. Follow your instructor's directions for the proper use of the spectrophotometer model you will use. Allow the instrument to warm up for 10 minutes before making measurements.

2. Obtain at least two colors (red, green, blue, or yellow) of diluted food dyes from your instructor.

3. Half-fill one spectrophotometer sample tube with distilled water. Use a separate sample tube for each of the dilute dye solutions. (Note: A 13- x 100-mm test tube without scratches works well in a Spectronic 20.)

4. When no sample tube is in the spectrophotometer no light strikes the detector. Adjust the instrument so that the transmittance reading is zero.

5. Set the wavelength selector to 400 nm. Insert the sample tube holding distilled water into the instrument after wiping the outside of the tube with a piece of tissue to remove water and

fingerprints. Now set the instrument to read 100% T, as the water is not absorbing any visible light. *Each time the wavelength of light is changed the 100% T position must be reset with the tube of water.* (This is necessary because the lamp does not have the same power at every wavelength.)

6. Remove the tube of water from the sample compartment of the spectrophotometer and set it aside. Take the first sample tube of dye, wipe its outside clean with tissue, and insert it into the sample compartment of the instrument. Read and record the %T in the Data Table on the Worksheet. If your instrument has a digital read-out switch on the display for absorbance and record this value as well.

7. Repeat step 6 for the second tube of dye.

8. Remove the tube of dye from the instrument. Reset the wavelength selector to 420 nm. Insert the tube of water and adjust the %T to 100%. (Do not adjust the 0 %T knob.)

9. Using the same tubes of dye as in steps 6 and 7, measure and record the %T of each sample.

10. Continue this way to take %T readings of both dye samples at 20 nm-increments until you have accumulated data for the 400–700 nm spectral range. Remember to reset the 100% T value with distilled water each time the wavelength is changed.

Determining the Relationship between Sample Concentration, Transmittance, and Absorbance

1. In this part of the experiment you will work with a single color of dye.

2. Label eight 15- x 150-mm test tubes #1, #2…#8.

3. Using a more concentrated solution of dye than you used for determining the absorption spectrum, add n drops of dye to tube #n; in other words, 1 drop of dye goes in tube #1 and 8 drops of dye are added to tube #8.

4. Add 10 mL of distilled water (measured with a 10-mL graduated cylinder) to the dye in each of the eight test tubes.

5. Stopper and gently shake each tube to mix the solutions uniformly.

6. Look back at the data you collected for the spectrum of the color of dye you are now using. Select the wavelength at which the %T was the least.

7. Set the spectrophotometer to read at the wavelength of minimum %T chosen in step 6. Set the 0% T reading with no tube in the sample compartment, and adjust the 100% T value with a tube of distilled water in the compartment.

8. Take another sample tube and rinse it with 1–2 mL of the dye solution from test tube #1. Discard this rinse. Now fill the sample tube about half-full with dye solution from test tube #1. Wipe the outside of the tube with a tissue.

9. Read and record the %T value of this solution in Data Table 2 on the Worksheet. If your instrument has a digital read-out, you can switch the display to absorbance and record this value as well.

10. Using the same tube for all sample solutions, repeat steps 8 and 9 for the other dye solutions in test tubes #2–8.

11. Ask someone else using the same food color as you to give you a sample of dye solution *without telling you the tube number*.

12. Determine and record the %T reading of the sample your classmate provided, using the rinse-fill-read procedure.

13. All the dye solutions may be flushed down the sink with water unless local or state regulations prohibit this disposal practice. If flushing is not permitted, pour the samples into the waste container provided by the instructor.

Pre-Lab Exercise A
Describe the purpose of the experiment in a few complete sentences of your own phrasing.

Pre-Lab Exercise B
Make a list of the chemicals and equipment you need for this experiment.

Pre-Lab Exercise C
Which color of visible light has the highest energy? Which has the lowest energy? Explain briefly.

Pre-Lab Exercise D
Explain why a patient's exposure to X-rays for medical purposes is carefully limited, but a much longer time can be spent in a MRI (magnetic resonance imaging) instrument without harm. The MRI uses radio waves for the diagnostic procedure.

Pre-Lab Exercise E
What is the absorbance of a solution that has 58% transmittance at a particular wavelength of light?

Pre-Lab Exercise F
Explain why red light can be used in a photographic darkroom where negatives are being developed, but white light cannot.

Pre-Lab Exercise G
Explain why the wavelength at which a solution has its smallest or least %T value is the also the wavelength at which the sample has the largest or greatest absorbance reading.

Pre-Lab Exercise H
What is the frequency of a wave of red light (wavelength 630 nm) traveling at 3.0×10^8 m/sec?

Pre-Lab Exercise I
Why does a piece of green-colored cloth appear black if it is illuminated under red light only?

Pre-Lab Exercise J

In Latin the word "ultra" means "beyond," while "infra" means "below." Ultraviolet and infrared radiation lie adjacent to visible light in the electromagnetic spectrum. What property of light do the modifiers "ultra" and "infra" refer to in the names speed, wavelength, and frequency? Explain.

Pre-Lab Exercise K

Ultraviolet light is sometimes referred to as "black light." Why?

Lab Worksheet   **Name:** _____   **Section:** _____

Part 1: Determining the Visible Spectrum of a Food Dye

1. In determining the visible spectrum of food dyes, you measured the %T values over a range of wavelengths. Record the data in Table 1 below. Leave the absorbance data column blank if you used an analog spectrophotometer.

Data Table 1: %Transmittance as a function of wavelength of light for two food dyes

Color of Dye →				
Wavelength of light, nm ↓	% Transmittance	Absorbance	% Transmittance	Absorbance

2. If you used an analog spectrophotometer, calculate the absorbance value corresponding to each measured %T reading and enter the result in Data Table 1 above.

3. Plot both the %T (left y-axis) and absorbance (right y-axis) data at each wavelength (x-axis) for one color of dye on the chart provided at the end of the Worksheet. Draw one smooth curve through the %T data and another smooth curve through the absorbance data points. Prepare a separate graph for the other dye. You may wish to make the plots with a program such as Microsoft Excel®. (Note: The data must be in contiguous columns and in ascending or descending order by wavelength to obtain a proper plot.)

4. On each spectrum indicate the color of the bands of visible light corresponding to the wavelengths listed in the table given in the introduction. That is, mark off the span of wavelengths that are red, orange, etc.

5a. Complete the following table based upon the spectrum you obtained for each dye.

Color of the food dye solution	Dye 1:	Dye 2:
Wavelength of minimum %T, nm		
Wavelength of maximum absorbance, nm		
Color of light at wavelength of maximum absorbance		
Wavelength of maximum %T		
Color of light at wavelength of maximum %T		

5b. Looking at the two visible spectra what relationship is apparent between %transmittance and absorbance at the same wavelength for each dye?

5c. Based on your results, is the color of the dye solution perceived by your eyes the same as the color of light that is transmitted or absorbed?

Part 2: The Relationship between Sample Concentration, Transmittance, and Absorbance

1. Record your results for the experiment in the spaces provided:

    Color of food dye used _____   Wavelength of light for analysis _____ nm

Data Table 2: Variation of transmittance and absorbance with dye concentration

Sample Tube	Number Drops of Dye	%Transmittance	Absorbance
#1			
#2			
#3			
#4			
#5			
#6			
#7			
#8			
Unknown	?		

2. If your spectrophotometer has an analog read-out, calculate the absorbance values corresponding to the measured %T data and enter the results in Data Table 2 above.

3. Using either the scale provided at the end of the Worksheet or a computer spreadsheet program, prepare the a graph that shows:
    a) the number of drops of dye in each sample on the horizontal axis;
    b) the %transmittance of each solution on the left vertical axis with a smooth curve or line drawn through the points; and
    c) the absorbance of each solution on the right vertical axis with a separate smooth curve or line drawn through those points.

4. The volume of the drops added to each tube is very small compared to the 10 mL of water added to each tube. Explain why the data on the horizontal axis could be labeled "concentration of dye in the sample solution."

5a. Which measured property, %transmittance or absorbance, exhibits a linear relationship with the number of drops of dye in the sample solution (or, dye concentration)?

5b. Does the property that varies linearly with the number of drops of dye show an increasing or decreasing dependence on the dye concentration?

5c. Summarize, in a simple statement, the relationship you have just deduced between %transmittance or absorbance and the concentration of the sample in the light beam.

6. Based upon your answers to questions 5a and 5b and your measured %transmittance of the dye solution obtained from a lab mate (the "unknown"), how many drops of dye are contained in the "unknown" solution?   Explain your reasoning briefly.

Now ask the person from whom you obtained the "unknown" dye solution to tell you the number of drops of dye actually present. Were you able to determine the correct number within 1 drop?

Why do you think a measurement of the %transmittance or absorbance of an "unknown" solution should be made on the same spectrophotometer at the same time the data for solutions of known concentration were collected?

7. Based on both parts of this lab exercise, describe a simple procedure that can be used to determine the concentration of a colored substance in a solution if you have access to some of the pure substance.

Visible Absorption Spectrum for Dye #1   Color = _____

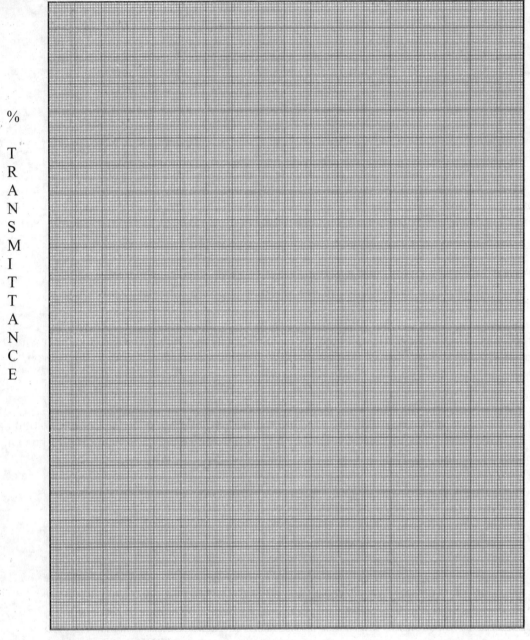

%

T
R
A
N
S
M
I
T
T
A
N
C
E

A
B
S
O
R
B
A
N
C
E

WAVELENGTH, nm

Experimenting with *The Chemistry of Everything*

Visible Absorption Spectrum for Dye #2   Color = _____

%

T
R
A
N
S
M
I
T
T
A
N
C
E

A
B
S
O
R
B
A
N
C
E

WAVELENGTH, nm

Variation of %Transmittance and absorbance with Concentration of Dye

Color of Dye = _____

%

T
R
A
N
S
M
I
T
T
A
N
C
E

A
B
S
O
R
B
A
N
C
E

Number of drops of dye in solution

Experimenting with *The Chemistry of Everything*

Introduction and Background

Matter can absorb and store heat. The absorbed thermal energy causes molecules in the liquid and gas state to move about more rapidly. In solids, atoms and molecules do not travel any significant distance, but instead "jiggle" or vibrate more rapidly about a fixed point.

The ability of a substance to store heat depends on its composition and physical state (gas, liquid or solid). The quantity of heat needed to raise 1 gram of any substance 1 °C is called its specific heat. If the object cools by 1 °C it also loses an amount of heat equal to the specific heat. For example, the amount of heat required to raise 1 gram of liquid water 1 °C is 4.184 Joules.

The total quantity of heat a substance has absorbed or released thus depends on what the object is (its particular specific heat), its mass, and the temperature change. Mathematically, this can be expressed as $Q = S \times m \times \Delta T$.
In this expression

Q = quantity of heat measured in Joules (J),
S = specific heat of a substance in Joules/(gram × °C),
M = mass of the substance in grams, and
ΔT = the temperature change = final temperature (T_f) – initial temperature (T_i).

For example, if 10 of g water is heated from 25° C to 50° C the quantity of heat absorbed is:
Q = $(4.184 \text{ J/(g·°C)}) \times 10 \text{ g} \times (50 - 25)°C = 1.0 \times 10^3$ J, or 1.0 kJ.

We can use the change in the temperature of a known mass of water to calculate the specific heat of another substance if it does not dissolve in water. If a hot object is dropped into a container of water, the heat lost by an object must equal the heat absorbed by the water. Once again, this can be expressed mathematically as $Q_{water} = - Q_{object}$. A positive sign indicates that heat is absorbed (flowing in), while a negative sign indicates that heat is being released (flowing out). *The transfer of heat is complete when both the water and the object reach the same final temperature, T_f.*

As above, the value of the heat lost and gained can be expressed in terms of the specific heats, masses, and temperature changes as follows:
$$Q_{water} = - Q_{object}$$

So, $S_{water} \times g_{water} \times (T_f - T_{i\ water}) = - S_{object} \times g_{object} \times (T_f - T_{i\ object})$.

If we want to determine the specific heat capacity of a substance, S_{object}, we need to design an experiment in which all the other values are known. The specific heat of water is given above; the masses of the water and object can be determined with a balance; and the temperatures are read with a thermometer. The major challenge is to ensure that nearly all the heat lost by the object is transferred to the water rather than the surroundings or a container.

On the "water" side of the experiment we can place a measured mass of water in a styrofoam cup (an insulated container) and take its initial temperature. We can heat the object being tested in an oven or bath, measure its initial temperature, and transfer the object to the water in the styrofoam cup. If the object is transferred quickly only a small amount of heat will be lost to the air.

This is the basic procedure you will use to determine the specific heat of blocks made from different types of metal. You will also examine how the specific heat of a metal correlates with its density and position in the Periodic Table of the Elements.

Working Safely

You will need to heat water to nearly boiling in this experiment. You can minimize the chance of being burned by using tongs or wearing insulated finger protectors to handle hot glassware, iron ware, and hot plates. If your lab uses a gas burner to heat water, set the height of the flame as low as possible and avoid brushing an article of clothing into the flame. Please remember that iron rings and hot plates will remain hot after the gas or electricity is shut off. If you do get burned, apply some cold water to the affected skin and seek medical attention.

A non-mercury thermometer is recommended for this experiment. If you must use a mercury thermometer, take care to avoid hitting the bulb with the metal blocks. When you are not using the thermometer, store it in your drawer or out of the way place where it can not be knocked on the floor. If the thermometer breaks and mercury is spilled, do not attempt to clean it up yourself. The instructor will have the proper tools to retrieve the spilled mercury.

Procedure

1. Obtain two identical 8-oz (250-mL) styrofoam beverage cups and nest one inside the other.

2a. Weigh and record the mass of the cups. Add about 50 mL of room-temperature water to the inner styrofoam cup. Determine the mass of the cups and water together. Subtract the mass of the empty cups to find the mass of the water. Record the mass of the water in the Data Table on the Worksheet.

OR

2b. Place the empty cups on the balance and press the "tare" button to zero out the weight of the cups. Add about 50 mL of room-temperature water to the inner cup. Read the mass of the water directly and record it in the Data Table.

3. Immerse a thermometer in the water in the styrofoam cup. (Support the thermometer so it will not tip the cup.) After 3 minutes record the initial temperature of the water in the Data Table on the Worksheet.

4. Obtain the block of metal from your instructor. If the metal has a label or code number, record this in the Data Table on the Worksheet.

5. Weigh the block of metal and record its mass in the Data Table. Use as many digits as can be read on the display of the balance.

6. The experiment works best if the metal block has either a hook attached or a hole bored through it. Attach a piece of plastic fishing line about 25–30 cm long to the block. The line will help you transfer the hot block quickly.

7.   Place a 400-mL beaker containing about 200 mL of water on a hot plate *OR* on a wire screen supported above a gas burner.

8.   Hang the metal block by the nylon line from a clamp attached to a ring stand so that the metal block is completely immersed in the water in the 400-mL beaker. The block should not be touching the walls of the beaker, but should be surrounded on all sides by water.

9.   Heat the water containing the metal block to a gentle boil. Once the water is boiling, keep the block in the hot water for about 3–5 minutes. [**Warning**: Keep the styrofoam cup away from the gas flame or surface of the hot plate. The cups are flammable, and they can melt on contact with the hot plate.]

10.   Carefully dip the thermometer in the hot water bath without touching the walls or bottom of the beaker. Note the temperature of the hot water. Assume that the metal block is at the same temperature, and record this in the Data Table.

11.   Turn off the gas or electric hot plate.

12.   Pick up the styrofoam cup with the water in one hand. With your other hand (or the assistance of a partner) lift the metal block out of the hot water bath and *immediately* transfer it to the styrofoam cup. Don't splash water out of the cup! Loosen the plastic line from the supporting clamp as quickly as possible *OR* swing the supporting clamp so that you can rest the cup on the bench with the metal block suspended in the water.

13.   Quickly insert the thermometer in the water in the styrofoam cup. The thermometer bulb should not touch the metal. Record the highest temperature attained by the water in the Data Table.

14.   Repeat the experiment two more times. After calculating the specific heat of the metal from each attempt, average the three results to get your "best" estimate of the metal's specific heat.

15.   If time permits, use a different metal block and follow steps 1–14.

Pre-Lab Exercise A
Describe the purpose of the experiment in a few complete sentences of your own phrasing.

Pre-Lab Exercise B
Make a list of the chemicals and equipment you need for this experiment.

Pre-Lab Exercise C

The equation given earlier for the quantity of heat transferred between water and a metal block is

$$S_{water} \times g_{water} \times (T_f - T_{i\ water}) = - S_{metal} \times g_{metal} \times (T_f - T_{i\ metal}).$$

Rearrange this equation to show that:

$$S_{metal} = \frac{- S_{water} \times g_{water} \times (T_f - T_{i\ water})}{g_{metal} \times (T_f - T_{i\ metal})}.$$

Pre-Lab Exercise D

Use the expression you obtained in Exercise C to solve this problem.

A block of metal weighing 60 g was heated to 100.0° C. The warm metal was quickly transferred to an insulated container holding 75 g of water at 15.0° C. The metal and water finally reach 18.6° C. If the specific heat of water is 4.184 J/(g·°C), what is the specific heat of the metal?

Pre-Lab Exercise E

Suppose 25 g of water initially at 100.0° C is added to 75 g of water originally at 15.0° C in an insulated container. What is the temperature of the water after mixing?

You can use the expression $S_{water} \times g_{water} \times (T_f - T_{i\ water}) = - S_{metal} \times g_{metal} \times (T_f - T_{i\ metal})$ to solve this problem as follows:

(1) Expand the equation by multiplying through the factors in parentheses on both sides of the equals sign.
(2) Collect the terms that involve T_f on one side of the equation.
(3) Perform the algebra to solve for T_f.
(4) Let the subscripts labeled "metal" refer to the hot water.

Pre-Lab Exercise F

A piece of marble weighing 51.5 g is heated to 80° C before it is placed in an insulated cup holding 75.0 g of water at 18° C. What is the final temperature reached by the marble and the water? The specific heat of marble is 0.88 J/(g·°C) and the specific heat of water is 4.184 J/(g·°C).

Hint: This problem is solved similarly to Exercise E.

Pre-Lab Exercise G

None of the mathematical expressions or calculations discussed earlier include a term related to the heat capacity of the styrofoam cup, yet the plastic container is in contact with the water used to make the experimental measurements. What (unstated) assumption is being made?

Pre-Lab Exercise H

A brick and a block of metal having the same mass are placed together in an oven. Both are removed at exactly the same time and set upon the same bench. The block of metal cools to room temperature much more quickly than the brick. Suggest an explanation for this observation in the light of what you have learned about heat capacity of materials.

Pre-Lab Exercise I

Winters in northern Minnesota routinely have temperatures well below 0° C, yet Lake Superior rarely completely freezes over. How is this possible? Relate your explanation to the discussion of heat capacity in this chapter. Hint: Lake Superior is the largest body of fresh water on Earth.

Lab Worksheet   Name: _____   Section: _____

1. Record your measurements in the appropriate spaces.

DATA TABLE   for Sample _____

	Trial #1	Trial #2	Trial #3
Mass of H_2O in styrofoam cup (grams) = g_{water} =			
Initial temperature of H_2O in styrofoam cup (° C) = $T_{i\ water}$ =			
Mass of metal block (grams) = g_{metal} =			
Temperature of hot water bath containing metal block (° C) = $T_{i\ metal}$ =			
Highest final temperature attained by H_2O in styrofoam cup after metal block added (°C) = T_f =			

DATA TABLE   for Sample _____

	Trial #1	Trial #2	Trial #3
Mass of H_2O in styrofoam cup (grams) = g_{water} =			
Initial temperature of H_2O in styrofoam cup (° C) = $T_{i\ water}$ =			
Mass of metal block (grams) = g_{metal} =			
Temperature of hot water bath containing metal block (° C) = $T_{i\ metal}$ =			
Highest final temperature attained by H_2O in styrofoam cup after metal block added (°C) = T_f =			

DATA TABLE   for Sample _____

	Trial #1	Trial #2	Trial #3
Mass of H_2O in styrofoam cup (grams) = g_{water} =			
Initial temperature of H_2O in styrofoam cup (° C) = $T_{i\ water}$ =			
Mass of metal block (grams) = g_{metal} =			
Temperature of hot water bath containing metal block (° C) = $T_{i\ metal}$ =			
Highest final temperature attained by H_2O in styrofoam cup after metal block added (°C) = T_f =			

2. Using the data from Trial #1 for the first metal block you tested, show how to calculate the specific heat of the metal. Express your answer with the correct number of significant figures and units. The specific heat of water is 4.184 J/(g·°C).

3. Record the specific heat values you calculated from each trial in the Results Table below. Also enter the average of the three trials for each metal.

Results Table

Sample	Specific Heat, Calculated from Trial #1	Specific Heat, Calculated from Trial #2	Specific Heat, Calculated from Trial #3	Average Specific Heat, from Trials #1, 2, 3

4. Your instructor will identify the metals you tested. Find the accepted value of the specific heat of your samples. Calculate the percentage error in your result using the formula

$$\text{percentage error} = \frac{(\text{observed result - true value})}{\text{true value}} \times 100\%$$

Take your average specific heat calculated in question 3 as the "observed result" and use the "accepted value" as the "true value." Calculate the percentage error for each sample of metal you tested. A positive % error means your result is larger than the accepted value, while a negative % error means your result was smaller than the accepted value.

Sample _____   % error =

Sample _____   % error =

Sample _____   % error =

The accepted values for the specific heats were obtained under more rigorously controlled conditions than were possible in your experiment. Look back at the procedure you used to calculate the specific heats. Even if you did everything correctly as described, there were several steps in the procedure where the measured values were possibly too small or too high. Identify several of these "errors."

Would the errors you just identified tend to make the calculated value of the specific heat smaller or larger than the "true value"? Explain.

5.   Listed below in alphabetical order are the specific heat and density values for several metals.[†]

Metal	Specific Heat , J/(g·°C)	Density, g/mL at 20° C
Aluminum	0.908	2.70
Cadmium	0.233	8.66
Chromium	0.460	7.15
Cobalt	0.433	8.72
Copper	0.389	8.95
Gold	0.132	19.33
Iron	0.473	7.87
Lead	0.128	11.35
Manganese	0.463	7.3
Nickel	0.456	8.92
Tin	0.23	7.32
Titanium	0.471	4.51
Tungsten	0.14	19.3
Vanadium	0.482	5.87
Zinc	0.39	7.14

Arrange the specific heat value of each metal according to the position of the element in the Periodic Table. Are any trends or patterns suggested by this arrangement of the data? Briefly summarize the trends in a sentence or two.

Do the density values follow a similar periodic trend? If yes, what is it?

[†] Data from "Lange's Handbook of Chemistry, 10th ed.," McGraw-Hill, 1969.

14	# A Trip to the Distillery
	## -Separating Liquids by Distillation-

Companion Sections in Waldron: Chapters 7.4, 7.5, 7.6, and 9.3

Introduction

Molecules in a liquid substance do not have a fixed location: They move about, colliding with each other and the walls of their container. Attractive forces between the molecules like hydrogen bonding, dipole-dipole forces, and non-polar interactions keep the liquid molecules in much greater proximity than in a gas.

The space above the surface of a liquid contains molecules of the substance in the gaseous state. Molecules in the liquid that have enough kinetic energy to overcome the intermolecular attractions pass into the vapor (gaseous) phase. As the temperature of the liquid increases a greater number of molecules vaporize. Some of the molecules in the gas state also return to the liquid form, or condense.

The *vapor pressure* is the pressure exerted by the gas phase above a liquid, and not surprisingly, the vapor pressure increases with temperature as more molecules vaporize. At the same temperature different liquids will have different vapor pressures. This reflects the differences in how readily compounds vaporize. For example, at 40° C acetone has a higher vapor pressure than toluene; this means acetone molecules pass from the liquid phase into the vapor phase more readily than do toluene molecules at 40° C. Thus, the concentration of acetone molecules in the vapor phase over liquid acetone at 40° C is greater than the concentration of toluene molecules in the vapor phase over liquid toluene at 40° C.

When a liquid is heated until its vapor pressure equals the atmospheric pressure, the liquid has reached its boiling point. *The boiling point of a liquid is the temperature at which its vapor pressure equals the atmospheric pressure*, which is assumed to be 1 atmosphere (760 mm Hg), unless stated differently. Heating a pure liquid at its boiling point provides the energy required to drive all the molecules into the gas phase, but does not raise the temperature of the liquid.

Now imagine a *mixture* of liquids A and Z that are miscible in all proportions (i.e., can be blended in any ratio to produce a solution). The vapor above a solution of liquid A and Z contains A and Z in the gas state. In a mixture of gases, each gas exerts its own pressure independently and in proportion to the number of its molecules that have vaporized. Thus, the total vapor pressure is the simple sum of the vapor pressure of each liquid. Here, this means we can write

$$\text{Pressure}_{total} = \text{Pressure}_A + \text{Pressure}_Z .$$

The liquid mixture of A and Z will boil at the temperature at which the total pressure ($\text{Pressure}_A + \text{Pressure}_Z$) equals the atmospheric pressure.

If a sample of the vapor above the liquid is analyzed and the composition of the two phases is compared, a very interesting fact emerges: *The vapor contains a greater fraction or proportion of the higher vapor pressure material than the liquid does*. In other words, there is relatively more of the lower-boiling component in the vapor than is present in the liquid. (Refer to Figure 14-1 below.)

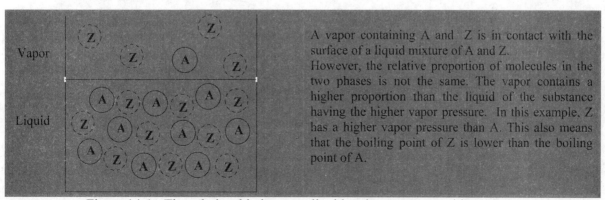

Figure 14-1: The relationship between liquid and vapor composition

Distillation is a purification process that separates the components of a mixture by differences in their vapor pressures. Distillation can be used to separate different liquids from each other or to separate liquids from solutions containing solids. For example, a dilute solution of ethyl alcohol in water obtained by fermentation of grain can be distilled to afford nearly pure alcohol. Potable water can be obtained by distilling sea water to leave the salt and other dissolved solids behind.

A distillation apparatus consists of:
(1) a boiling flask ("the pot") in which the solution to be separated is heated,
(2) a space in which the hot vapors are collected and the temperature is measured ("the stillhead"),
(3) a tube in which the hot vapors are cooled to liquid ("the condenser"), and
(4) a container ("the receiver") in which the liquid being distilled ("the distillate") is collected.

The glassware may also include a "fractionating column" placed between the boiling flask and the stillhead. Inside the fractionating column are small pieces of wire, glass, or other surfaces upon which the hot vapors can partially cool. Some of the vapors condense and run down the column back in to the boiling flask. The vapors that cool off the easiest are those of the higher boiling compound in the vapor mixture. By elongating the path the vapors must travel, an even higher concentration of the lower boiling vapors reach the stillhead to be collected. A sketch of a distillation apparatus with a fractionating column is shown below.

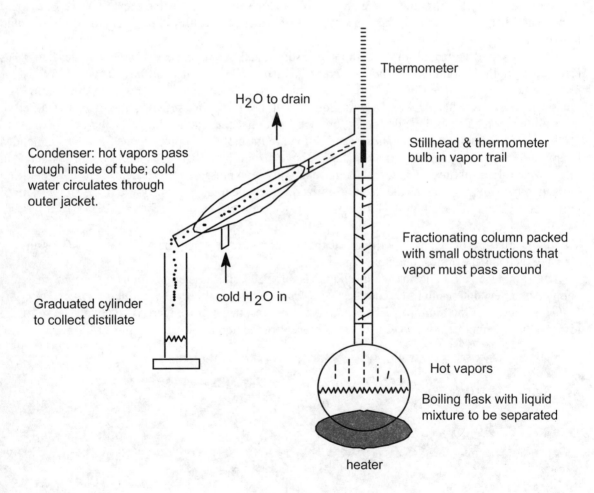

Figure 14-2: Schematic of a distillation apparatus with a fractionating column

Once the mixture is heated to boiling in the flask, hot vapors begin to ascend inside the distillation apparatus, much like smoke goes up the chimney of a fireplace. As we saw earlier, the vapors just above the boiling liquid are more concentrated in the low-boiling component of the mixture than the liquid phase. However, there is yet another process at work that helps separate the mixture. Since only the boiling flask is externally heated, the rising hot vapors come in contact with cooler glass surfaces. Some heat is transferred from the vapor to the glass, and a portion of the hot vapor condenses. This liquid flowing back down into the flask is mostly the higher-boiling component of the mixture, while the ascending vapor is enriched in the lower-boiling liquid. This cycle of partial condensation that occurs along the entire path length of the vapor provides the extra separation of the mixture.

The hot vapor passes over the thermometer bulb immediately before it enters the condenser. A counter-current of cold water flowing against the outside wall of the condenser absorbs the heat of vaporization, converting the vapor leaving the top of the column to a liquid of essentially the same composition. The distillate (liquid leaving the condenser) can then be collected. As long as the temperature at the stillhead does not change, the composition of the distillate does not change. When the temperature reaches the boiling point of the component that is being purified, it can be collected in a receiving flask by itself. Thus, the temperature at the stillhead indicates not only how the distillation is progressing, but also what is being collected in the receiver.

Background

In this experiment you will separate a mixture of methanol (boiling point 64° C) and water (boiling point 100° C) using several configurations of a distillation apparatus:

      (a) simple distillation—no fractionating column is used;

      (b) fractional distillation with an empty column;

      (c) fractional distillation with a packed column.

There are a number of ways of completing the experiment. Your instructor may have you and a partner perform two or three variations of the distillation. Or, several students may each perform a different distillation variation and share their findings. The idea is to collect sufficient data to enable you to compare the result of separating the same mixture under several different circumstances.

The progress of each distillation is monitored by recording the volume of distillate received and the temperature of the vapor at the stillhead as it enters the condenser. A graph of this data shows how well the separation of the liquids proceeds. Imagine that you started with 100 mL of 1:1 by volume methanol and water. If the distillation perfectly separated the two liquids you would obtain 50 mL of methanol boiling at 64° C and then the temperature would jump up to 100° C as water began to distill. The temperature-versus-volume graph would look like Figure 14-3a below.

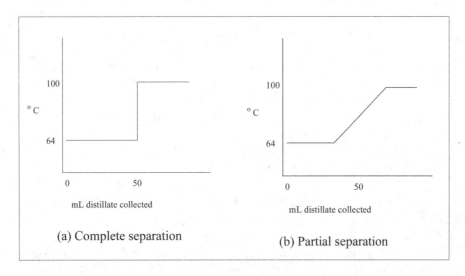

Figure 14-3: Graphs of temperature versus volume of distillate collected

On the other hand, a distillation that provides less than 50 mL of pure methanol and then a mixture of water and methanol before giving some pure water would have a temperature-versus-volume graph similar to Figure 14-3b. Over the portion of the graph where the curve slopes upward, the temperature climbs as the composition of the distillate includes a greater fraction of water.

In a worst-case scenario, a graph like those in Figure 3 would continuously rise during the course of the distillation, indicating that little useful separation of the liquids was occurring.

Working Safely

Methanol (also called methyl alcohol or wood alcohol) is toxic if ingested; it can not be metabolized by the body and eliminated like ethyl (grain) alcohol. Drinking methanol can cause blindness or death. Do not remove any of the alcohol from the lab.

Methanol can enter the body by being absorbed through the skin or by inhalation of its vapors. Although you are not at serious risk of harm in this experiment, wear gloves or wash spills off your skin right away with cold water. Keep containers of the alcohol closed when not in use, and check that the connections between pieces of your distillation apparatus are leak-proof.

Dispose of any waste methanol in the container provided by your instructor. Do **not** pour methanol down the sink drain.

Methanol is flammable, and when it is ignited the flames may be hard to observe. The distillation should be performed using electric heating devices only.

Procedure

1. The exact type of glassware available varies from lab to lab, so please be aware that your instructor may need to modify some of these instructions. Steps 3–21 assume that your lab is using glassware with ground glass joints and heating with an electric mantle regulated by a variable transformer.

2. Your instructor will tell you what type of distillation to perform. Working with a partner makes the experiment easier to carry out.

3. Securely clamp a 100-mL round bottom flask by its neck to a ring stand about 6 inches above the bench. Pour 20–25 mL of methanol and an equal volume of distilled water into the flask, *OR* pour 40–50 mL of pre-mixed 1:1 by volume methanol-water into the flask. Add several boiling stones to the flask as well.[†]

4a. If you are performing a *simple distillation*, do nothing and go directly to step 5a.

4b. If you are using an *empty fractionating column*, insert the lower male joint into the neck of the boiling flask. Clamp the column at its upper end in a truly vertical position. Go to step 5b.

4c. If you are using a *packed fractionating column*, loosely fill the column with wire mesh, pieces of glass tubing, or glass beads provided by your instructor. [**Note**: The packing has to be supported at the bottom of the column so it will not spill out.] Clamp the column at its upper end in a truly vertical position. Go to step 5b.

5a. Attach the stillhead to the joint in the neck of the boiling flask. The connection for the thermometer should be pointing straight up in the air.

[†] Boiling stones are insoluble pieces of porcelain or other material containing small air-filled channels. When the stone is heated, the air escapes as a fine stream of bubbles that rise through the liquid and break the surface tension to promote smoother boiling.

5b. Attach the stillhead to the joint in the top of the fractionating column. The connection for the thermometer should be pointing straight up in the air.

6. Moisten the bulb of the thermometer with some water. Slowly and gently slip the thermometer through the rubber connector that closes the opening at the top of the stillhead. (Hold the thermometer close to the piece of rubber as you feed it through the connector.) Wipe any moisture off the bulb with a piece of tissue.

7. Attach the rubber thermometer adapter and thermometer to the top of the stillhead. Adjust the position of the thermometer bulb so that the top of the bulb is just even with the lower opening in the angled tube of the stillhead. (See Figure 14-2.)

8. Attach tubing to the two hose connectors on the condenser. The tubing needs to be long enough to reach the faucet and the drain or trough on the lab bench.

9. Insert the joint of the angled arm of the stillhead into the corresponding joint in the condenser. Use another clamp attached to a ring stand to loosely support the condenser so that the joints stay pressed together and the condenser does not fall. (If you apply too much pressure to the clamp on the condenser, the angled joint of the stillhead will fracture!)

10. Place a small funnel in the mouth of a 50-mL graduated cylinder. Position the funnel and cylinder under the exit spout of the condenser.

11. Attach the hose connected to the lower inlet of the condenser to the faucet. Lead the tube connected to the upper hose connection of the condenser into the sink.

12. Position a heating mantle under the boiling flask so that the bottom of the flask touches the mantle. Connect the mantle to the transformer, and then plug the transformer into the electrical outlet.

13. Before starting the distillation have your instructor check and approve the set-up of your apparatus.

14. Begin to pass a slow stream of water through the condenser. Apply just enough water pressure to make water flow uphill and exit the drain tube.

15. Turn on the transformer and adjust the voltage setting according to your instructor's advice (about 50% power is good to start).

16. Be patient: It will take a while for the liquid to warm up to boiling. If nothing seems to be happening in about 5 minutes, check that the transformer is plugged into the outlet and that the electrical connections are secure between the mantle and transformer.

17. Once the alcohol-water mixture begins to boil, you should notice a ring of vapor and liquid begin to rise up inside the neck of the flask into the stillhead (simple distillation) or the column (fractional distillations). When the vapor hits the thermometer bulb the temperature will surge upward.

18. In the Data Table on the Worksheet record the temperature at which the first drop of distillate appears in the graduated cylinder as "0" mL. Thereafter, record the temperature at the stillhead for each 2- or 3-mL increase in the volume. Let the distillate continue to fall into the cylinder.

19. As the distillation progresses, the liquid remaining in the flask will boil at a higher temperature. If the stillhead temperature falls before most of the liquid has distilled from the flask, you need to increase the transformer power to the mantle.

20. Continue collecting temperature-volume data until at least 35 mL of distillate has boiled over. Then turn off the electricity to the mantle. When the mantle is cool enough to handle, you can lower it.

21. Once the liquid in the flask is no longer boiling, turn off the water to the condenser. After the residue in the boiling flask cools to room temperature you can pour it and the distillate into the waste container provided by your instructor.

Pre-Lab Exercise A
Describe the purpose of the experiment in a few complete sentences of your own phrasing.

Pre-Lab Exercise B
Make a list of the chemicals and equipment you need for this experiment.

Pre-Lab Exercise C
Explain why the vapor pressure and boiling point of a liquid are inversely related. That is, why does a liquid of low vapor pressure have a high boiling point?

Pre-Lab Exercise D
Is it possible to separate two different liquids that have the same boiling point by distillation? Why or why not?

Pre-Lab Exercise E
Suppose that you distill a mixture of water and methanol at sea level and then repeat the experiment in a lab in the mountains one mile above sea level. Do you expect to see any difference in the boiling points? If yes, what is the difference? Why does this happen? **Hint**: Look back at the definition of the boiling point.

Pre-Lab Exercise F
Why does the temperature at the stillhead gradually rise during a distillation?

Pre-Lab Exercise G
Based on the material in the introduction, why might you expect a simple distillation to be less efficient at separating water and methanol than a fractional distillation?

Pre-Lab Exercise H
Why should it be easier to separate water from salt water (aqueous NaCl) than from a mixture of water and methanol?

Pre-Lab Exercise I
Why is distillation an expensive process for obtaining drinking water from sea water?

Lab Worksheet   Name: _____   Section: _____

1. Record the volume and temperature data from your distillation experiment(s) in the table below.

Simple Distillation		Empty Column		Packed Column	
Distillate Total Volume (mL)	Temperature (° C)	Distillate Total Volume (mL)	Temperature (° C)	Distillate Total Volume (mL)	Temperature (° C)

2. Plot the data from the table above on the scale provided at the end of the exercise. Set the vertical axis = temperature and the horizontal axis = total distillate volume. It will be easier to compare the results from the three distillations if the data from all three experiments are plotted on the same graph. You can either use different colored ink or assign different markers to the data in each experiment (e.g., x, o, and +). Draw a smooth curve to connect the data points for each distillation. Alternatively, you can enter the data into a computer spreadsheet and plot the results.

3. Use the graphical presentation of your data to answer the following questions. Provide some justification or explanation of your answer in each case.

a. Which distillation produced the largest volume of liquid within 5° C of the boiling point of pure methanol?

b. Which distillation gave the most efficient separation of methanol and water?

c. Do the results of your experiments suggest that more partial condensation of the hot vapors occurs in a fractional distillation with a packed column than in an empty fractionating column?

d. Is an empty fractionating column more efficient at separating water and methanol than a simple distillation? Why should this be so?

e. If you suppose that any liquid boiling between 62° C and 67° C is pure methanol, what percentage of the original methanol could be recovered in each of the distillations by changing receivers after the temperature rises above 67° C?

f. Which distillation took the most time to perform, on average, once the liquid in the flask began boiling? Assuming the same heating rate was used in each case, what accounts for the difference in time required to carry out the distillation?

g. Based on the results of these experiments, which distillation method would you use to obtain the greatest percentage of relatively pure methanol in the shortest amount of time?

TEMPERATURE AT STILLHEAD °C

© Pearson Custom Publishing

TOTAL VOLUME OF DISTILLATE COLLECTED (mL)

Introduction

Anyone who watches television is familiar with the commercials for Mountain Dew and with the crazy antics of the dudes who "do the Dew." Undoubtedly the exploits of these young men are induced by an over-consumption of caffeine, the organic chemical that gives Mountain Dew and many other products the "kick" or "pick-me-up" so many of us seem to crave.

According to one version of history, ancient monks in the Middle East noticed that goats eating the berries of the coffee bush were especially frisky and active. The monks' religious routine required that they awake several times during the night and early morning for prayer. One of the monks (no doubt a sleepy head) decided to drink a brew made from the beans to facilitate wakefulness during night prayers. Apparently, the experiment had a stimulating result, for the popularity of drinking coffee spread throughout Europe.

Today, caffeinated beverages are both extremely popular and highly profitable. Numerous over-the-counter medications also contain caffeine to give the user a slight "lift," helping one to feel that the medication is efficacious. Over the last fifty years, the safety of consuming significant amounts of caffeine has been the subject of numerous studies that have reached conflicting conclusions. For most people, ingesting "moderate" amounts of caffeine does not appear to be a serious health threat. Even so, a significant fraction of the population does not tolerate well the effects of caffeine; pregnant women and people with high blood pressure and heart disease are often advised to restrict their caffeine intake. Others do not consume caffeine for religious reasons. As a result, there is also a profitable market for decaffeinated coffee, tea, and other beverages.

So how do the food and pharmaceutical industries manage to take caffeine out of naturally occurring sources in order to add it to synthetic concoctions? A relatively simple technique called *extraction* works well, and it can be used for many compounds besides caffeine.

Background

Liquids that do not dissolve each other are said to be *immiscible*. When liquids are immiscible the intermolecular forces of attraction between like molecules are very many times more powerful than those attracting unlike molecules. As a result, the liquids segregate and form distinct layers when placed in the same container, with the more dense liquid settling to the bottom. For example, if water and hexane are poured into the same baker the bottom layer is water (density 0.99 g/mL at 20° C), while the hexane floats on top (density 0.66 g/mL at 20° C). Water is a polar compound in which the individual H_2O molecules interact strongly by forming hydrogen bonds.

Two water molecules associated by a hydrogen bond (indicated by the dashed line).

Hexane, on the other hand, is a non-polar hydrocarbon; individual hexane molecules associate by relatively weak intermolecular forces.

The non-polar C-C and C-H bonds in hexane render the entire molecule non-polar and hydrophobic.

Let us put the discussion in more general terms and see how the immiscibility of liquids relates to the separation technique of extraction.

Imagine having a beaker containing a solution of compound Z dissolved in Liquid 1. Suppose that a less dense immiscible Liquid 2 is then added to the beaker. What happens?

You probably quite correctly predicted that two layers form in the beaker with Liquid 2 floating atop Liquid 1, as shown in the sketch below.

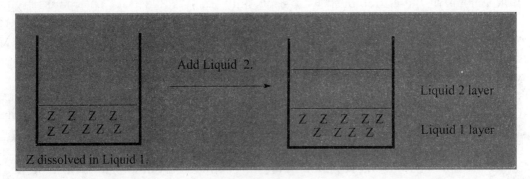

But imagine that compound Z also dissolves in Liquid 2. As molecules of Z move around in Liquid 1, some will reach the interface or boundary between the two liquids. There is nothing to prevent Z migrating across the interface. Molecules continue moving between the two phases, but at some point the rate at which Z enters and leaves Liquid 1 and Liquid 2 becomes the same. Then equilibrium is reached and the relative amount of Z in each phase no longer changes, and Z ends up partitioned or distributed between the two liquid layers.

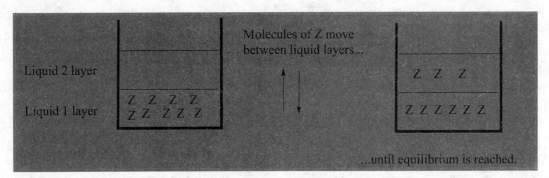

In this example, the ratio of Z between Liquid 2 and Liquid 1 is in the ratio 3:6 .

Extraction can now be defined in more formal language as a separation process in which a substance is partitioned between two immiscible liquids. Imagine that Liquid 1 contained other materials besides Z. If Z preferentially passed into Liquid 2, the upper layer could be separated from the lower layer and evaporated to recover some pure Z.

To recover a greater quantity of Z from the mixture in Liquid 1 another portion of clean Liquid 2 could be added and mixed. When equilibrium is reached the same ratio of Z is again found distributed between the liquids: 1:2 (which of course equals 3:6).

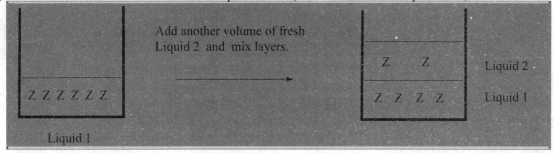

The process of adding fresh Liquid 2 to remove additional Z from the solution in Liquid 1 can be repeated as often as desired until as much Z as is practical has been recovered.

By now you may be thinking, "wouldn't it have been easier to simply evaporate Liquid 1 from the original solution to recover Z?" That's a fair question. During the laboratory synthesis of an organic compound, the product may be obtained mixed with other chemicals in an aqueous solution. By carefully selecting the liquid for extraction the desired product can be "fished out" of the mixture preferentially—simply evaporating the water would leave everything behind mixed with the product. Thus, extraction is most useful when one compound in a mixture is much more soluble in a particular immiscible liquid than the other components.

Mountain Dew is a water solution containing sugar or artificial sweetener, caffeine, citric acid, juice, carbon dioxide, other flavorings, preservatives, and dye. In order to undo the Dew by extracting the caffeine, we need a solvent that is immiscible with water and dissolves caffeine in preference to the other chemicals in the solution. The ideal solvent also should be cheap, not very toxic or hazardous to the environment, and have a low boiling point so that it is easily separated from the caffeine. Often it is not possible to find an ideal solvent. In our experiment the solvent is ethyl acetate, an ester made from acetic acid (in vinegar) and ethyl alcohol; it dissolves caffeine, but very little of the other materials found in Mountain Dew.

$$CH_3\text{-}CH_2\text{-}O\text{-}\overset{\overset{\textstyle O}{\|}}{C}\text{-}CH_3$$ *ethyl acetate :* less dense than water; boiling point 77° C; biodegradable; dissolves caffeine; but flammable

For many years chloroform, $CHCl_3$, was considered the ideal solvent to extract caffeine because $CHCl_3$ dissolves caffeine better than just about any other solvent, it is cheap, its boiling point is 61° C, and the liquid is not flammable. Unfortunately, it is now known that long exposure to $CHCl_3$ promotes the development of cancer, and chloroform which escapes into the atmosphere promotes depletion of the ozone layer. Although ethyl acetate does not dissolve caffeine as well as chloroform and it is flammable, these disadvantages are far less serious than those of $CHCl_3$.

In this experiment you will extract the caffeine from a small volume of Mountain Dew and use the mass of recovered caffeine to estimate how much stimulant is ingested by someone drinking a can or bottle of the brew.

> **Working Safely**
>
> Ethyl acetate is flammable. No gas burners or other ignition sources should be used in the lab room during this experiment! Vapors of ethyl acetate are mildly irritating. The extraction should be performed in a well-ventilated area, preferably in a fume hood. Place waste ethyl acetate in the disposal container provided by your instructor; it must not be flushed down the drain.
>
> Do not consume any of the Mountain Dew or caffeine used in this lab. Unless local and state law forbids it, the left-over pop and caffeine can be flushed down the sink.

Procedure

1. Weigh 9–10 g of NaCl (ordinary table salt is acceptable) into a 250-mL beaker.

2. Measure 50 mL of regular (sweetened with corn syrup) Mountain Dew with a graduated cylinder. Empty the pop into the beaker containing salt.

3. Stir the mixture until all the salt dissolves. (This will take a little while.) Enough NaCl is being mixed with the pop to form a nearly saturated solution in order to reduce the solubility of the caffeine in the aqueous layer.

4. Support a 125-mL separatory funnel on an ring clamped to a ring stand as shown in Figure 15-1a. Turn the stopcock valve so that no liquid can drain from the funnel.

5. Add 20 mL of ethyl acetate to the separatory funnel, and stopper the flask.

6. Gently shake the separatory funnel to mix the liquid layers. *Reminders*: (a) hold the stopper in while shaking the funnel; (b) relieve some of the pressure by pointing the delivery stem up and away from anyone else before opening the valve as shown in Figure 15-1b.

7. Close the delivery valve, and then support the separatory funnel upright on the ring stand. Allow the mixture to stand undisturbed for about 5 minutes or until a clear, sharp boundary appears between the two liquid layers.

8. Remove the stopper from the funnel. Place the 250-mL beaker that contained the Mountain Dew under the delivery tip. Open the valve to draw out the lower yellow layer. When the liquid boundary reaches the lower narrow neck of the funnel, partially close the valve so the liquid flow can be controlled precisely. Close the valve just as the boundary line enters the valve.

9. Temporarily set the beaker of pop aside. Now drain the upper ethyl acetate layer into a dry 125-mL Erlenmeyer flask. Stopper it, label it, and save it.

10. Close the valve on the delivery stem and pour the beverage mixture back into the separatory funnel. Add another fresh 20-mL portion of ethyl acetate to the funnel.

11. Repeat steps 6, 7, and 8.

12. Drain the ethyl acetate in the funnel into the Erlenmeyer flask containing the first 20-mL extract.

13. A small amount of water gets carried along with the ethyl acetate solution of the caffeine, even if you can not see any. This water needs to be "sponged up" or removed by "drying the solution." Add about 3 g of anhydrous sodium sulfate (Na$_2$SO$_4$) to the ethyl acetate solution. Gently swirl

Fig 15-1a: Separatory funnel basics	Figure 15-1b: Using a separatory funnel
1. Support the separatory flask on an iron ring clamped to a rod.	1. Grasp the neck of the flask and apply light pressure against the stopper to keep the funnel sealed.
2. The valve is *closed* when the handle on the stopcock is *parallel to the bench*.	2. Elevate the delivery tube above the liquid level inside the funnel. Open the stopcock valve briefly to vent any vapor. Do not point the delivery tube at your face or at a neighbor.
3. Always keep a beaker under the tip of the funnel to catch any liquid that drips or leaks.	
4. The stopper must be removed in order for liquid to drain from the funnel.	3. Gently shake or "slosh" the liquids together.
	4. Close the valve. Support the funnel upright on the ring until the liquids are clearly separated.
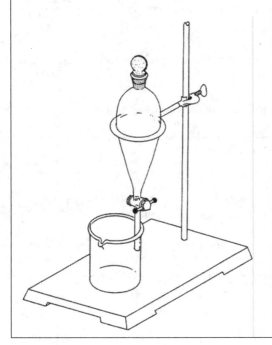	5. Remove the stopper and drain the lower layer into a flask or beaker. 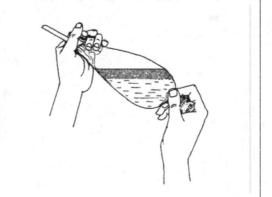

Figure 15-1: The separatory funnel

the Erlenmeyer flask—if any water is present the loose powder will collect into a near-solid mass on the bottom of the flask. The white solid is a crystal that contains 10 water molecules for every one Na_2SO_4. If the white solid appears "runny" you need to add about 2–3 g more Na_2SO_4 and swirl again to completely absorb the moisture.

14. The caffeine extracted from Mountain Dew must now be separated from the ethyl acetate. Carefully *decant* (pour off) most of the ethyl acetate from the crystalline $Na_2SO_4 \cdot H_2O$ through a funnel into a 100- or 125-mL distilling flask.

15. Add about 2 mL of clean ethyl acetate to the solid left in the Erlenmeyer and swirl the flask a few minutes to rinse out any remaining caffeine extract. Decant the rinse into the distilling flask without transferring any solid. Add several boiling stones to the flask.

16. Assemble the apparatus shown in Figure 15-2. You may use a stopper in the neck of the flask in place of the thermometer.

17. Heat the ethyl acetate to boiling with an electric heating mantle or hot water bath as your instructor directs. Collect the nearly pure ethyl acetate that distils in a small beaker. *The liquid remaining in the boiling flask contains the caffeine.* Stop the heating when about 5 mL of liquid remains in the boiling flask. Pour the distilled ethyl acetate into the designated recycling container.

18. Allow the warm caffeine-ethyl acetate solution in the boiling flask to cool to near room temperature. Meanwhile, weigh a clean, dry 25-mL Erlenmeyer flask or beaker and record its mass on the Worksheet.

19. Use a long disposable pipette and bulb to transfer the ethyl acetate solution in the boiling flask to the pre-weighed flask or beaker. Place a boiling stick in the flask. Evaporate the remaining ethyl acetate on a hot plate (low to moderate heat) in the hood When solid first starts to appear on the walls of the flask, remove the flask from the heat using "hot fingers," thermal gloves, or tongs.

20. When the flask is at room temperature weigh it and the contained caffeine on the same balance as before, recording the total mass on the Worksheet.

21. Dispose of the Mountain Dew and caffeine according to your instructor's directions.

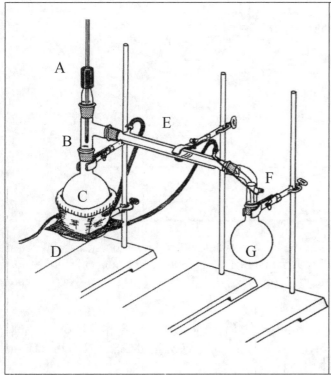

The apparatus in your lab may be slightly different from that shown here.

A is a thermometer inserted through a rubber and glass connector. You may replace this assembly with a simple glass stopper.

B is the stillhead.

C is the boiling flask containing the ethyl acetate and caffeine solution plus several boiling stones.

D is an electric heating mantle supported on an iron ring clamped to the stand.

E is the water condenser. Water enters through the lower hose on the right and exits to the sink through the upper hose at the left.

F is the delivery tube.

G is the flask for collecting the evaporated ethyl acetate.

Figure 15-2: Simple distillation apparatus for partial removal of ethyl acetate from caffeine

Pre-Lab Exercise A
Describe the purpose of the experiment in a few complete sentences of your own phrasing.

Pre-Lab Exercise B
Make a list of the chemicals and equipment you need for this experiment.

Pre-Lab Exercise C
Extraction is used in many kitchens every day, though no separatory funnel or immiscible liquids are needed. Explain how brewing coffee from grounds or tea from tea leaves is an extraction.

Pre-Lab Exercise D
Suppose that a cool sample of tea was extracted three times with ethyl acetate. Explain why each extraction should be done with a clean portion of ethyl acetate in order to successfully extract the maximum possible amount of caffeine. In other words, what is wrong with reusing the very same portion of ethyl acetate for all three extractions?

Pre-Lab Exercise E
Imagine that 1000 mg caffeine was dissolved in 200 mL of water. When this solution was extracted with 20 mL of $CHCl_3$, the chloroform was found to contain 400 mg of caffeine. Suppose that the 600 mg of caffeine remaining dissolved in the 200 mL was extracted again with 20 mL of clean $CHCl_3$. How many milligrams of caffeine would you predict to be found in the second chloroform extract?

Pre-Lab Exercise F
What is the molecular formula of caffeine?

Pre-Lab Exercise G
Show how to calculate the molar mass of caffeine.

Pre-Lab Exercise H
If someone drinks a large-sized cup of really strong coffee, he or she might consume 300 mg of caffeine. How many moles caffeine are contained in 300 mg?

Pre-Lab Exercise I
The two parts of this question review the topic of "intermolecular forces."

(a) What atom groups in the caffeine molecule are important in making the compound soluble in water?

(b) Why is caffeine also soluble in a polar organic solvent like ethyl acetate?

Lab Worksheet   Name: _____   Section: _____

1. Record the following data from your experiment:

    Mass of the empty flask = _____

    Mass of the flask and caffeine after the ethyl acetate evaporated = _____

2. What is the mass of caffeine in milligrams that you recovered from the 50-mL sample of Mountain Dew ?

3. List the mass of caffeine recovered from 50 mL Mountain Dew by at least four other different students:
    Result 1 = _____ mg   Result 3 = _____ mg

    Result 2 = _____ mg   Result 4 = _____ mg

    Combining your own result and the four other students' results, what is the average number of mg of caffeine extracted from the pop sample?

4. Suppose that the average value for the mass of recovered caffeine is close to the actual amount of caffeine actually present in the beverage.

a) If a person drinks an entire 12-oz can of pop and 1 fluid ounce equals 29 mL, how many milligrams of caffeine are ingested based on your answer to question 3?

b) Suppose you go to a fast food restaurant and have a "super-sized" 20-oz serving of Mountain Dew .   How many milligrams of caffeine have you consumed?

5. Suppose that you had extracted the 50-mL sample of Mountain Dew three times with 15 mL of ethyl acetate. Explain why you would have recovered slightly more caffeine overall than with two extractions.

    Why would the last extraction have contained the smallest mass of caffeine of the three extractions?

Introduction

Some winters seem to last forever—especially if you live in Minnesota like the author; the coldest temperature on record here is about –60° F. Even so, there are colder places, such as Antarctica (lowest reported temperature is near –130° F). Yet lower temperatures are found in outer space. In January 2005 the space probe *Huygens* landed on Titan, one of Saturn's moons, where the surface temperature is a less than balmy –269° F. These chilling facts raise a very real question: Is there a lower limit to how cold it can get?

The behavior of gases provides us a tool to answer this question. You probably have seen a gas-filled balloon shrink in the cold and expand when it warms up. The warmer gas molecules move faster and collide more forcefully with the walls of the balloon. At constant atmospheric pressure this results in expansion of the volume of the gas (and hence the balloon). Thus, the volume of a gas is proportional to its temperature, or $V \propto T$. (The symbol $\propto$ means "is proportional to.")

Now imagine cooling a gas like helium until there is no empty space between the atoms: The volume of the gas will get smaller and smaller and approach zero. The temperature at this point is called *absolute zero*, the lowest possible temperature. Actually, the volume of the gas will not become zero since mass takes up space. A gas also will liquefy when cooled enough; for example, helium liquefies at –269° C. Molecules continue to move about within the liquid state, but at absolute zero, all movement of atoms ceases.

The relationship between the volume and temperature of a gas appears to be linear. This means that a consistent change in temperature causes the volume to change in the same proportion, so that a graph of volume versus temperature should be a straight line. Thus, it is not necessary to be able to actually reach absolute zero in order to determine the numerical value of this temperature. If we measure the volume of a gas at various temperatures and graph the results, the straight line can be extended, or extrapolated, to the temperature at which the volume theoretically becomes zero.

Background

The apparatus for this experiment is fairly simple: We need a sample of gas kept at constant pressure, a way to measure the gas volume, and the ability to vary and to measure the temperature of the gas. With air as the gas, the experiment can be performed at atmospheric pressure using the equipment shown in Figure 16-1.

The "empty" Erlenmeyer flask is filled with air trapped in the space above the water in the burette. The tubing leading from the lower outlet of the burette and the bottle is filled with water. The level of water in the burette is adjusted by raising and lowering the reservoir. Since the external atmospheric pressure will not change significantly during your experiment, the pressure acting down on the open end of the reservoir, on the water, and on the air trapped inside the flask remains constant. Once the height of the water reservoir is set, the level of water in the burette will change only in response to changes in the volume of gas trapped in the flask. If the air volume in the flask shrinks, the water level in the burette rises by an equal volume. Similarly, if air expands in the flask, it pushes down on the water in the burette. The temperature of the gas is adjusted by immersing the flask in a warm or a cold bath. All that remains is to take readings of the gas volume from the water level at various temperatures.

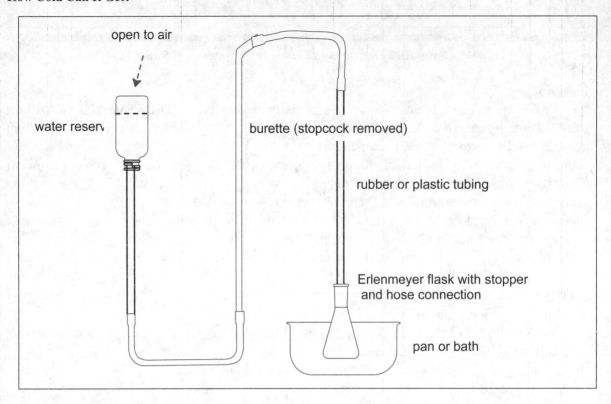

open to air

water reserv

burette (stopcock removed)

rubber or plastic tubing

Erlenmeyer flask with stopper
and hose connection

pan or bath

Figure 16-1: Apparatus[†] for measuring gas volumes at different temperatures
(Clamps and ring stands are not shown for simplicity.)

-The water reservoir ("reserv") is a plastic bottle with the bottom removed. A stopper with a connecting
tube is inserted in the mouth, or a dispensing bottle with a delivery tip connects to the tubing.
-A standard student burette with the stopcock valve removed is used to measure the gas volume.
-The connections between the tubing and the glass are short pieces of rigid plastic or glass tubing fitted
into serum caps or stoppers.

[†] This same apparatus is used for the synthesis of nitrogen gas in the next experiment.

Procedure
*No dangerous chemicals are used in this experiment, but you should wear safety glasses or goggles
in case any glassware breaks.*

1. Although the apparatus may be set up for you when you come to lab, steps 2–5 assume that you
    will assemble the equipment yourself. You can skip to step 6 if the apparatus is pre-assembled.

2. Support the plastic bottle used as a water reservoir on an iron ring or a funnel stand clamped to a
    vertical rod. Attach a length of hose to the delivery tip of the bottle or the tube in the stopper.

3. Insert the stoppers with the connecting tubes into both ends of a 50-mL burette. Clamp the burette
    upright to a rod with the "0 mL mark" at the top. Connect the loose end of the hose from the
    water reservoir to the tube at the "50 mL" end of the burette.

4. Pour room-temperature water into the open end of the bottle. Check that no air bubbles are in the hose or the burette. Gently tap the burette or move the water bottle up and down to dislodge bubbles, if any are present. The level of water in the burette and bottle should be the same if there are no blockages in the hose.

5. Attach another hose to the tube in the stopper at the top of the burette, and connect the other end to the stopper in the mouth of a 125-mL Erlenmeyer flask. Loop the hose over a support clamp so that the tube hangs without pinching shut under its own weight when the flask rests on the bench.

6. Make sure that all the hose connections are tight. Once you close off the Erlenmeyer flask and start making measurements, the apparatus must remain sealed. Clamp the flask in a fixed position in the bath for each experiment.

7. Adjust the amount of water and the height of the bottle so that water rises up inside the burette to about the 20-mL mark..

8. Allow the apparatus to stand for about 5 minutes at room temperature. Record the water bath temperature and the water level in the burette under "Experiment 1" in the Data Table on the Worksheet. Read the volume at the meniscus (the low point of water surface in the tube). Although the burette can be read to two decimal places, in this experiment an estimate to the nearest 0.1 mL is adequate.

9. For the remaining experiments, fill the bath with water at the temperature ranges listed below and clamp the flask so that it is immersed in the water as much as possible. Place a thermometer in the bath and wait about 5 minutes for the gas to reach the same temperature as the bath before recording the temperature and burette water level for each experiment in the Data Table on the Worksheet.

   (a) For Experiment 2 use "tepid" water (about 30–40° C).

   (b) For Experiment 3 use "hot" water (about 50–60°C). ***Warning****: Water at or above 50° C can cause burns very quickly if it is spilled on the skin!*

   (c) For Experiment 4 use "very hot" water (about 80–95° C). ***Warning****: Water at or above 50° C can cause burns very quickly if it is spilled on the skin!*

   (d) For Experiment 5 fill the bath with "cold" water (about 10–15° C).

   (e) For Experiment 6 add ice to the bath water to bring the temperature to 0–5° C.

Pre-Lab Exercise A
Describe the purpose of the experiment in a few complete sentences of your own phrasing.

Pre-Lab Exercise B

Make a list of the equipment you need for this experiment.

Pre-Lab Exercise C

Charles's Law is usually written $V_1/T_1 = V_2/T_2$, where V_1 is the volume of gas at an initial temperature and V_2 is the gas volume when the temperature changes to a second value. Why must the temperature be measured on the absolute zero (or Kelvin) scale for calculations using Charles's Law?

Pre-Lab Exercise D

The ideal gas law is $PV/nT = $ constant, where P is the gas pressure, V is the gas volume, n gives the number of moles of gas, and T is the gas temperature. Suppose that you have a balloon filled with gas. Assuming that the balloon does not leak and that the gas pressure does not change, show how to obtain Charles's Law (given in Exercise C) from the ideal gas law.

Pre-Lab Exercise E

Look back at the sketch of the experimental apparatus in Figure 16-1. Suppose that the water reservoir were not open to the atmosphere and that you heated the gas in the Erlenmeyer flask. What property or properties (P, V, n, T) of the gas would change? Why might the stopper pop out of the flask under these circumstances?

Pre-Lab Exercise F

If you were going to be driving your car in the desert in the middle of summer, why might you want to let some air out of the tires before going a long distance?

Lab Worksheet   **Name:** _____   **Section:** _____

1. For each of your experiments record the bath temperature in column B and the corresponding water level in the burette in column C. Experiment 1 is performed at room temperature. Leave columns D and E empty for now.

   Data and Results Table

A	B	C	D	E
Experiment	Bath Temperature (° C)	Water Level (mL)	Volume Change (mL)	Volume of Trapped Air (mL)
1			0	125
2				
3				
4				
5				
6				

2. The values in column D are calculated from the water levels in column C.
   "Experiment 1" is the reference or comparison point.
   The result for Experiment 2 = the water level in Experiment 2 – the water level in Experiment 1. For example, if the water level in Experiment 1 was at 20.0 mL in the burette and then at 35.0 mL for Experiment 2, the "Change in volume" for Experiment 2 in column D would be 35.0 – 20.0, or +15.0 mL. (This means the volume of air expanded by 15.0 mL.)   If the water level in Experiment 3 were at 17.0 mL when it had been 20.0 mL for Experiment 1, then the change in volume would be 17.0 – 20.0, or –3.0 mL . (This means the volume of air shrank by 3.0 mL.)

   Complete the calculations for column D for Experiments 2–6.

3. Now you need to find the actual volume of air trapped between the water and flask at each temperature. When the air in the flask expands, the water level in the burette is pushed down to a higher volume reading. When the air contracts, the water level in the burette rises to a smaller reading. The actual air volume in each of the other experiments is the original air volume at room temperature (125 mL) plus the change in volume observed, or 125 + the entry in column D.

   Complete the calculations needed for the column E in Experiments 2–6.

   Before proceeding further, take a moment to ask yourself if the calculated numbers in column E make sense when you compare them with the temperatures in column B. That is, do the volumes in column E change with the temperature in column B in the correct direction?

4. Now you are ready to make a graph of the volume and the temperature data. There are two ways to go about this.

Method 1: Graphical Extrapolation

Prepare a plot of your temperature and volume data on the graph scale provided on the last page of this experiment.

(a) Display the temperature values on the horizontal axis aligned with the longer edge of the graph paper. This axis should read from $-325°$ C to $+100°$ C.

(b) Show the volume of trapped gas on the vertical axis, with values ranging from 0–150 mL.

(c) For each experiment, mark a point on the graph corresponding to the data in columns B and E.

(d) Use a ruler or another straight edge to draw a straight line that most closely passes through all the points you marked. Extend the line backwards until it intersects the horizontal axis. The temperature at which the line crosses the axis is your estimate of absolute zero—the temperature at which molecular motion ceases. What is your estimate?

(e) Look up the accepted value for absolute zero on the Celsius scale. What is it?

(f) Calculate the percentage error in your result using the definition

$$\text{percentage error} \quad = \quad \frac{\text{observed result - accepted value}}{\text{accepted value}} \quad \text{x} \ \ 100\%$$

Scientists use a "percentage error" to compare how large the difference is between the observed result and "accepted value" relative to the size of the measurement being made.

(g) Suggest some ways in which the procedure or equipment could be changed that would make your calculated value for "absolute zero" closer to the "accepted value."

Method 2: Numerical Extrapolation on a Spreadsheet

If you have experience working with a computer spreadsheet program like Microsoft Excel® you can quickly graph your data and estimate absolute zero.

(a) Open the spreadsheet program and enter the gas temperatures in the first column and the corresponding volumes in the second column. Be sure to list the values either in increasing or decreasing order (or use the "sort" function to do this.)

(b) Select the cells containing your data in step (a). Call up the "chart wizard" and choose the scatter graph using the option which gives a smooth line through the data points.

(c) Label the axes, and close the wizard dialogue box.

(d) When the graph is displayed, point the mouse at the line and click the right mouse button. In the dialogue box select the option which calculates and displays a "trend line." Choose the option "forecast backwards" (extrapolated) until the line intersects the horizontal axis.

(e) Choose the program option to display the formula of the line. The equation will be in the form
> Y (volume) = slope • X (temperature) + constant.

You are estimating absolute zero as the temperature at which the volume of gas theoretically becomes zero, so you can write the equation as 0 = slope•X + constant. Use the values the program finds for the slope and the constant to solve the equation for X, the Celsius value of absolute zero. Show how to calculate the estimated value of absolute zero from your results.

(f) Look up the accepted value for absolute zero on the Celsius scale. What is it?

(g) Calculate the percentage error in your result using the definition given above in Method 1 under step (f).

5. Suppose that there was a small hole in the tubing used to connect the Erlenmeyer flask with the burette in this experiment. Explain why your measurements might show that there is no change in gas volume with a change in the gas temperature.

6. Based on your estimated value for absolute zero, what would be the formula used to convert between temperature on the Celsius and Kelvin scales?

7. Use your volume and temperature readings from Experiment 1 and Charles's Law to calculate the expected volume of the trapped air at the temperature you used in Experiment 3. How closely do the calculated and the observed volumes of the trapped gas compare?

8. Would a 500-mL Erlenmeyer flask be too large to use in this experiment with a 50-mL burette? Why or why not?

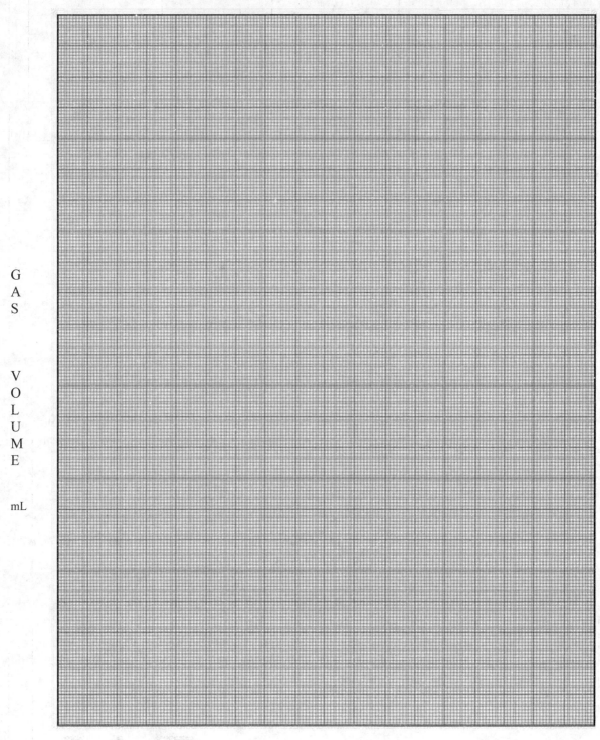

© Pearson Custom Publishing

GAS VOLUME mL

TEMPERATURE OF GAS, ° C

Graph of gas volume versus temperature of gas from data and results table

Experimenting with *The Chemistry of Everything*

Companion Sections in Waldron: Chapter 8.3-6

Introduction

Nitrogen was first isolated from air after the oxygen had been consumed by a combustion reaction. When experiments like this were performed by the early chemists of the 18th century, the exact composition of the atmosphere was not known. The scientists of the time did not realize that the nitrogen obtained by using up oxygen was also mixed with small amounts of argon, carbon dioxide, and other gases. Since these gases are heavier than nitrogen, the measured density of nitrogen was larger than the true value.

Later on, chemists prepared samples of pure nitrogen gas as the product of a chemical reaction. The gas obtained this way was observed consistently to have a lower density than "nitrogen" obtained by removing oxygen from air. From this very simple set of observations, chemists were led to discover the other gases which make up the earth's atmosphere.

Today, liquefied air is distilled to separate the nitrogen from the other gases. Liquid nitrogen itself is an important cryogen (low-temperature coolant) needed for superconducting magnets like those at the heart of a magnetic resonance imaging instrument (MRI) used in hospitals. The gas inside incandescent light bulbs is nearly pure nitrogen. (Can you suggest why N_2 is used instead of air?)

In this experiment you will prepare a sample of pure nitrogen gas by a chemical reaction, collect the gas and measure its volume by displacing water. From the volume, pressure, and temperature of the nitrogen you will calculate the number of moles of nitrogen gas obtained with the help of the ideal gas law. Last, you will be able to compare the expected and the actual amounts of nitrogen you collect.

Background

The word equation for the reaction used to make nitrogen gas is

Sulfamic acid + sodium nitrite → sodium hydrogen sulfate ("bisulfate") + nitrogen + water.

(Sulfamic acid and sodium bisulfate are found in a number of bathroom tile and toilet cleaning products. Sodium nitrite is used to preserve packaged meat by preventing the growth of microorganisms which release botulinum toxin.)

The reaction equation written with chemical formulas is

$$H_3SO_3N + NaNO_2 → NaHSO_4 + N_2 + H_2O.$$

The equation written using structural formulas is

The reaction is very quick: Nitrogen gas is evolved as soon as sulfamic acid and sodium nitrite are mixed in water; the entire reaction is complete in one minute. If all the nitrogen gas is to be captured and measured, the apparatus must be designed so that reaction does not start until the gas can be contained. A simple sketch of the equipment used is shown on the next page in Figure 17-1.

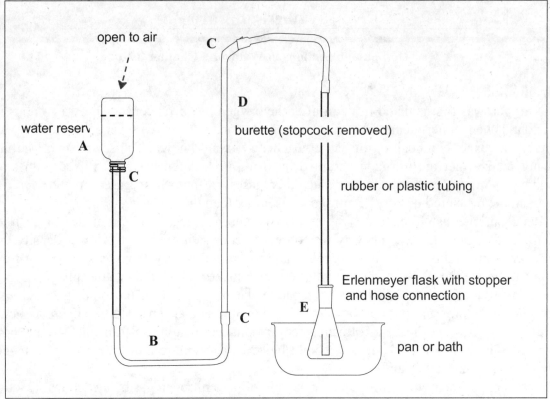

Figure 17-1: Apparatus for synthesis and capture of nitrogen gas
(Clamps and ring stands are not shown for simplicity.)

- **A** is a plastic dispenser bottle with the bottom removed. Partially filled with water, its height is adjusted to set the water level in the gas burette. **A** is called the "leveling bulb."
- Rubber or plastic Tubes **B** connect the pieces of apparatus.
- Connectors **C** are short pieces of rigid plastic or glass tubing fitted into serum caps or stoppers.
- **D** is a standard student burette with a removable stopcock valve assembly.
- **E** consists of a 125-mL stoppered flask which contains the water and the sulfamic acid. The small vial contains the sodium nitrite. (The pan is not strictly needed, but can be used to contain spills, if any.)

Notice that the only place the apparatus is open to the atmosphere is at the top of the water reservoir. As long as the pressure of the gas trapped in the space between the Erlenmeyer flask and the water in the burette is the same as the atmospheric pressure, the level of water in the burette and the reservoir will be the same.

When the reaction makes nitrogen in the Erlenmeyer flask, the newly-formed gas pushes water out of the burette into the reservoir until the interior pressure once again equals the atmospheric pressure. The volume of gas produced is determined by measuring the volume of space over the water in the burette before and after the reaction. This works because nitrogen is not significantly soluble in water. By reading the barometric pressure we know the pressure of the N_2 inside the gas burette.

Knowing the volume of gas inside the burette, the actual barometric pressure, and the temperature of the apparatus we can calculate the moles of nitrogen gas from the ideal gas equation as

$$\# \text{moles} = \frac{P \cdot V}{R \cdot T} .$$

P represents the pressure in atmospheres, *V* stands for the volume of gas in liters, *T* is the temperature on the Kelvin or absolute scale, and *R* is the gas constant, 0.0821 L·atmosphere/(mole·K).

The volume of gas generated contains not only nitrogen, but also a small amount of water vapor. Although it is possible to account for the moles of water vapor mixed with the nitrogen, we will ignore this correction to make our calculations simpler; the error in the final result is less than 3% by doing so.

Once you have experimentally determined the number of moles of nitrogen produced, you can compare it to the moles of nitrogen expected from the balanced equation. This calculates the percentage yield of nitrogen in the reaction.

Working Safely

Wear safety glasses or goggles while performing the experiment. You may wish to wear gloves while weighing out the chemicals needed.

Sulfamic acid is a skin irritant and may cause a burn if left in contact with the skin. Sodium nitrite is also a potential irritant. Transfer both solids using a spatula or paper. Neither compound should be ingested. Remember to keep your fingers out of your eyes, mouth, ears, and nose during lab to avoid accidental contact with the chemicals.

The liquid remaining in the flask at the end of the reaction is acidic. Pour this waste into a container provided by your instructor.

Procedure

1. Although the apparatus may be set up for you when you come to lab, steps 2–7 assume that you will assemble the equipment yourself. You can skip to step 6 if the apparatus is pre-assembled.

2. Support the plastic bottle (the kind which comes with a screw cap and a delivery tip) used as a leveling bulb on an iron ring or a funnel stand clamped to a vertical rod. Attach a length of hose to the delivery tip of the bottle.

3. Insert the stoppers with the connecting tubes into both ends of a 50-mL burette. Clamp the burette upright to a support with the "0 mL" mark at the top. Connect the loose end of the hose from the leveling bulb to the tube at the "50 mL" end of the burette.

4. Pour room-temperature water into the open end of the leveling bottle. Adjust the amount of water and the height of the bottle so that water rises up inside the burette to between the "0" and "10 mL" lines. Check that no air bubbles are in the hose or the burette. If there are, gently tap the burette or move the leveling bulb up and down to dislodge the bubbles. The level of water in the burette and the bottle should be the same if there are no blockages in the hose.

5. Attach another hose to the tube in the stopper at the top of the burette. Connect the other end to the hose inserted into the stopper that fits the mouth of a 125-mL Erlenmeyer flask. Near the top of the burette loop the hose over a support clamp so that the tube hangs without pinching shut under its own weight. The hose needs to be long enough to allow the Erlenmeyer flask to sit on the bench without a pinch or a crimp closing the hose.

6. Obtain a small a 4-mL shell vial and make sure that it can easily pass through the open neck of the Erlenmeyer.

7. Pour about 10 mL of water into the Erlenmeyer flask. Practice sliding the vial down the side wall of the flask so that the vial lands upright without being immediately filled by water. Being able to accomplish this feat is actually one of the more demanding skills needed for the experiment to succeed!

8. You may want to perform the experiment once or twice for practice before attempting to collect data for your calculations.

9. Weigh 0.080–0.090 g of sodium nitrite ($NaNO_2$) into the small vial. You will need to either "tare" the vial on the balance or record its mass before and after adding the sodium nitrite. The vial does not need to be completely dry inside, but wipe the outside of the vial dry before weighing it. Record the actual mass of $NaNO_2$ used in the Data Table on the Worksheet.

10. Weigh 0.15–0.16 g of sulfamic acid (H_3SO_3N) into the 125-mL Erlenmeyer flask. Only the outside of the flask needs to be dry. Record the actual mass of the sulfamic acid in the Data Table. Then add about 10 mL distilled water to the sulfamic acid, and swirl the flask gently to dissolve the solid.

11. You are almost ready: Check once more that the tubing is connected snugly to the top and bottom of the burette. Raise or lower the water bottle to bring the water level inside the burette between the "0" and "10-mL" marks.

12. This step demands your skill and concentration. Cautiously tip the Erlenmeyer flask part way on its side so that you can slide the vial of $NaNO_2$ into the flask without the solid spilling into the aqueous sulfamic acid or having water rush into the vial. (Of course, you do not want to pour the water and sulfamic acid out of the flask either!)

13. Attach the stopper and tubing connecting the flask to the top of the burette so that the hose is not pinched closed.

14. Read and record the water level in the burette in the Data Table on the Worksheet. To do this, align the meniscus (the curve at the bottom of the water level) with the mark on the scale. The scale is subdivided in tenths of a milliliter and you can estimate the distance between two lines; thus, the volume can be measured to two decimal places.

15. Be alert—things will happen very quickly now! Swiftly but gently tip the Erlenmeyer flask upright and swirl it so that all of the $NaNO_2$ dissolves and reacts with the sulfamic acid. Almost immediately the level of the water is pushed down in the burette. Read the new water level right away and record it in the Data Table. That's it, the reaction is over!

16. Read the barometric pressure and record it in the Data Table.

17. Measure the room temperature at your bench station and record it in the Data Table.

18. Empty the acidic solution in the Erlenmeyer flask into the waste container. Rinse the vial and the Erlenmeyer with some distilled or deionized water.

19. You can repeat the experiment starting at step 9 after adjusting the water level in the burette.

Pre-Lab Exercise A
Describe the purpose of the experiment in a few complete sentences of your own phrasing.

Pre-Lab Exercise B
Make a list of the chemicals and equipment you need for this experiment.

Pre-Lab Exercise C
This experiment demonstrates how scientists use the ideal gas law to calculate a single property of a gas when the other properties are not changing during the experiment. That is why we need to know the value of the gas constant, R, in $PV = nRT$. What terms in the ideal gas equation have the units L, atm, mole, and K?

Pre-Lab Exercise D
Barometric pressure is usually reported in units of mm Hg (millimeters mercury). If atmospheric pressure is 760 mm Hg at sea level, what is the pressure of the atmosphere when the barometer falls to 730 mm Hg? Show your work and express the answer with the proper number of significant digits.

Pre-Lab Exercise E
An "empty" 250-mL beaker is full of air. How many liters of air are in the beaker?

Pre-Lab Exercise F
Suppose that you were using the ideal gas equation in the form PV/RT to calculate the number of moles of gas in a balloon at 0° C. What problem would occur with your calculation if the temperature used in the equation was on the Celsius scale?

Pre-Lab Exercise G

If a gas is at $-15°$ C, what is its temperature on the Kelvin scale? Show your work.

Pre-Lab Exercise H

How many moles of $NaNO_2$ are there in 3.5 g of $NaNO_2$ if the mass of one mole is 69.00 g? Show your work and express the answer with the correct number of significant figures.

Pre-Lab Exercise I

How many moles of sulfamic acid are there in 4.50 g if one mole contains 97.09 g sulfamic acid? Show your work and express the answer with the correct number of significant digits.

Lab Worksheet   **Name:** _____   **Section:** _____

1. Record your measurements from the experiment in the Data Table below. Space is provided for up to three trials.

   Data Table

	Trial #1	Trial #2	Trial #3
Mass of sodium nitrite, NaNO$_2$ (grams)			
Mass of sulfamic acid, H$_3$SO$_3$N (grams)			
Water level in burette before reaction (mL)			
Water level in burette after reaction (mL)			
Barometric pressure in lab (mm Hg)			
Temperature at lab bench (°C)			

2. The equation for the reaction producing nitrogen is

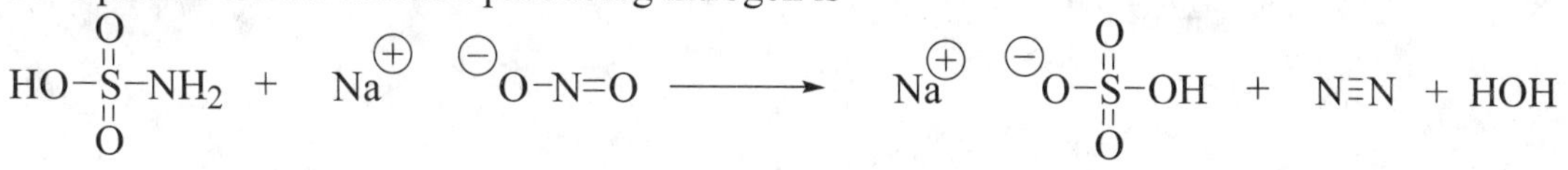

$$\underset{\underset{O}{\|}}{\overset{\overset{O}{\|}}{HO-S}}-NH_2 \;+\; Na^{\oplus} \;\;^{\ominus}O-N=O \longrightarrow Na^{\oplus} \;\;^{\ominus}O-\underset{\underset{O}{\|}}{\overset{\overset{O}{\|}}{S}}-OH \;+\; N\equiv N \;+\; HOH$$

   Is this equation balanced? That is, are the number and kinds of atoms shown to the left of the arrow (reactants) the same as those shown to the right of the arrow (products)?

   For every 1.0 mole of sulfamic acid reacted, how many moles of sodium nitrite must react?

3. The molar mass of sodium nitrite (NaNO$_2$) is 69.00. How many grams of NaNO$_2$ are contained in 1.0 mole of this compound?

   Show how to calculate the number of moles contained in the mass of NaNO$_2$ used in Trial #1. Give the answer with the correct number of significant digits. Also enter this value in the Results Table at the bottom of the next page. (If you performed the experiment several times, calculate and enter the corresponding values in the Results Table as well.)

4. The molar mass of sulfamic acid (H$_3$SO$_3$N) is 97.09. How many grams of H$_3$SO$_3$N are contained in 1.0 mole?

   Show how to calculate the number of moles contained in the mass of H$_3$SO$_3$N used in Trial #1. Give the answer with the correct number of significant digits. Also enter this value in the Results Table. (If you performed the experiment several times, calculate and enter the corresponding values in the Results Table as well.)

5. Compare the number of moles of sodium nitrite ($NaNO_2$) and of sulfamic acid (H_3SO_3N) used in Trial #1. What is the maximum number of moles of nitrogen (N_2) that can be produced from this combination of reactants? Asked differently, what is the theoretical maximum number of moles of N_2 that can form in Trial #1? (Chemists call this maximum number of moles of a product the *theoretical yield*.) Enter the value for each trial in the Results Table below. Repeat the process for any other trials.

6. The difference in water levels in the burette before and after the reaction is completed represents the volume of nitrogen gas produced at the barometric pressure and temperature in your lab. Show how to calculate the number of liters of gas produced in Trial #1. Enter this value (and those for any other trials) in the Results Table.

7. Show how to convert the barometric pressure in mm Hg units to atmospheres for Trial #1. Record this value in the Results Table. Do the same for any other trials.

8. Convert the lab temperature from degrees Celsius to kelvins for Trial #1, and write the number in the Results Table. Do the same for any other trials.

9. You now have all the experimental values in the correct units to calculate the number of moles of nitrogen produced in your experiment from the measured volume, pressure, and temperature. If the ideal gas constant R = 0.0821 L·atm/(mole·K), calculate the number of moles of nitrogen produced in Trial #1. Write the result with the correct number of significant figures in the Results Table. Do the same for any other trials.

Results Table

	Trial #1	Trial #2	Trial #3
Moles of sodium nitrite, $NaNO_2$			
Moles of sulfamic acid, H_3SO_3N			
Theoretical yield of N_2 (in moles)			
Volume of N_2 produced (in Liters)			
Pressure in lab (atmospheres)			
Temperature at lab bench (kelvins)			
Actual amount N_2 obtained (in moles)			
Percentage yield of N_2			

10. Chemists use the *percentage yield* to express the efficiency of a synthesis. The definition is

$$\text{Percentage Yield} = \frac{\text{amount of product obtained}}{\text{theoretical yield of product}} \times 100\%$$

Calculate the percentage yield of nitrogen obtained in each of the experimental trials; show work for Trial #1 below and enter the yield into the Results Table. Report the percentage yields for any other trials.

11. Most likely you did not get a 100% yield of N_2 in your experiment. Assuming that you performed the experiment correctly, suggest some reasons why you did not collect all the N_2 expected from the balanced reaction equation.

12. Suppose that you performed your experiment at sea level and then repeated it exactly at 1 mile above sea level. Would you expect the volume of gas collected to be greater, less, or the same as at sea level? Why?

13. If the room temperature were 27° C, would you expect the volume of gas collected from the same amounts of sodium nitrite and sulfamic acid to be greater, less, or the same on a day when the lab was only 18° C? Assume that the atmospheric pressure was the same both days.

14. Many cleaning products contain sulfamic acid as an active ingredient. Suppose that you wanted to analyze a sample of a cleaner to determine how much sulfamic acid was present. How could you use the apparatus in this experiment and a supply of sodium nitrite to analyze the cleaner?

Companion Sections in Waldron: Chapters 12.1, 12.2, 12.3, and 7.7

Introduction

Here is a little brain teaser for you: How are the terms *fat*, *oil*, *bio-diesel*, and *soap* related to each other? Yes, soap can help you clean up after a greasy day's work in the garage at the truck stop, but think harder. Here's a hint: Think about *esters*. Stumped? Then read on.

An ester is a organic compound formed when a carboxylic acid and an alcohol react to expel a molecule of water:

carboxylic acid	alcohol		ester	water

$$R-\overset{\overset{\text{O}}{\|}}{C}-O-H \;\; + \;\; H-O-R^* \;\longrightarrow\; R-\overset{\overset{\text{O}}{\|}}{C}-O-R^* \;\; + \;\; HOH$$

R and R* represent the rest of the molecule.

Esters of low molecular weight are often pleasant smelling, volatile liquids responsible for the characteristic odor of some fruits and plants. When the list of ingredients on a package of candy, soft drink, or other treat reports "artificial flavoring added," most likely an ester made in a lab is responsible for the enhancement of your experience.

High molecular weight esters are neither volatile nor especially "fruity" smelling. Plant and animal cells make a class of esters derived from the alcohol *glycerol* as a energy storage depot. Since each molecule of glycerol contains three alcohol groups, three molecules of carboxylic acids can combine with it to make a *triester*, which is usually called a *triacylglyceride* or triglyceride.

$$\underset{\begin{array}{c}\text{glycerol, or}\\\text{1,2,3-propanetriol}\end{array}}{\underset{\begin{array}{ccc}|&|&|\\\text{OH}&\text{OH}&\text{OH}\end{array}}{\text{CH}_2-\text{CH}-\text{CH}_2}} \quad + \; 3 \;\; \underset{\text{"fatty acid"}}{R-\overset{\overset{\text{O}}{\|}}{C}-O-H} \quad\longrightarrow\quad R-\overset{\overset{\text{O}}{\|}}{C}-O-\overset{\overset{\displaystyle\text{CH}_2-\text{O}-\overset{\overset{\text{O}}{\|}}{C}-R}{|}}{\underset{\underset{\displaystyle\text{CH}_2-\text{O}-\overset{\overset{\text{O}}{\|}}{C}-R}{|}}{\text{CH}}} \quad + \; 3 \;\; \text{H}_2\text{O}$$

triacylglyceride; Note: R usually does not have the same structure in each group.

Triacylglycerides are synthesized in cells with the help of enzymes as catalysts. The long hydrocarbon chains (represented as "R" is the structures above) are non-polar and hydrophobic, so triacylglyerides typically dissolve in solvents of low polarity such as hexane, ether, or chloroform.

People recognized and used triacylglyerides long before their chemical structures and properties were understood; these substances were (and are still) commonly referred to as *fats* or *oils*. Fats are solid at room temperature, while oils are liquids at room temperature. Fats more commonly contain single-bonded carbon atoms in the "R" group and are termed *saturated*—the maximum amount of hydrogen is found bonded to each carbon. On the other hand, oils are often *unsaturated* because the long chains from the carboxylic acid group contain one or more double bonds between carbons. Unsaturated oils can be chemically treated with H_2 gas and a catalyst in a chemical factory to make the triglyceride a solid. This is the process that has been used for many years to make margarine from corn oil; the same process is used to obtain the "partially hydrogenated oils" named in lists of ingredients on packages of prepared foods.

Unsaturated oils are most often found in plants (e.g., olive, soybean, or corn) and fish, whereas saturated fats are found in animal flesh. By now you have read and heard about the health issues surrounding the relative proportions of saturated and unsaturated fat in our diets. This experiment does not focus on the health and nutrition issues, but rather on a very old commercial use of triglycerides.

You may recall from earlier history courses how settlers living in frontier regions of the American continent got along without a local supermarket. When livestock were slaughtered, the pioneers saved the fat deposits surrounding internal organs for grease to lubricate wooden wagon wheels and to make candles and soap. Soap making or *saponification* involves a significant amount of chemistry.

Like any ester, triacylglycerides can be broken down into their constituent alcohol and carboxylic acid(s). One way to do so involves heating the ester or triacylglyceride with sodium hydroxide (lye) or potassium hydroxide (potash) in water.[1]

a fat from three different fatty acids   glycerol

$$CH_2-O-\overset{\overset{O}{\|}}{C}-R^1$$
$$R^2-\overset{\overset{O}{\|}}{C}-O-CH \qquad + \quad 3 \text{ NaOH} \quad \xrightarrow[\text{heat}]{H_2O} \quad HO-CH_2-\overset{\overset{OH}{|}}{C}H-CH_2\text{-}OH \quad +$$
$$CH_2-O-\overset{\overset{O}{\|}}{C}-R^3$$

$$Na^{\oplus} \quad {}^{\ominus}O-\overset{\overset{O}{\|}}{C}-R^1 \quad \text{and} \quad R^2-\overset{\overset{O}{\|}}{C}-O^{\ominus} \quad {}^{\oplus}Na \quad \text{and} \quad Na^{\oplus} \quad {}^{\ominus}O-\overset{\overset{O}{\|}}{C}-R^3$$

sodium salts of three different fatty acids = a mixture of soaps

"Soap" is the mixture of the sodium or potassium salts of the carboxylic acids that results from the hydrolysis. When the saponification mixture is cooled, curds of soap separate from the liquid; the solids can be skimmed off, poured into molds, and left to harden. (Glycerol is highly soluble in water.) Soap made this way is not especially good for one's complexion since it also contains some of the strong base!

But how does soap make it possible to get stuff clean? The explanation is not hard to come by once we remember the saying "like dissolves like" (Waldron Chapter 7.7).

---

[1] You might wonder where the pioneers got their supply of NaOH or KOH. Wood was the major fuel of the day, which led to the accumulation of ash. When wood ash is mixed with water, the NaOH, KOH, Na_2CO_3, and K_2CO_3 are extracted from the insoluble waste.

The salts of the fatty acids produced in the saponification reaction are ionic compounds, but the ionic group represents a very small portion of the entire substance; the much larger hydrocarbon chain is non-polar and hydrophobic. Consider the sodium salt of stearic acid, the C18 fatty acid:

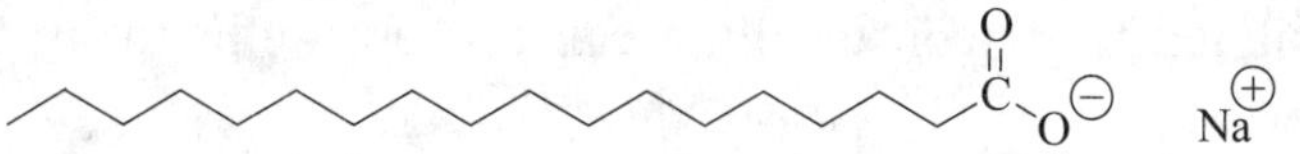

also drawn as

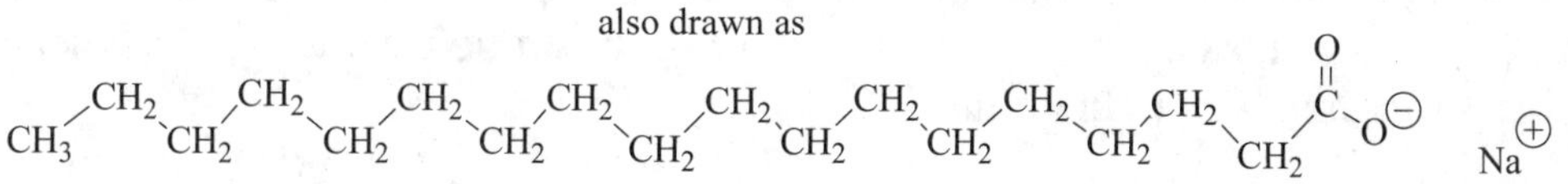

The ionic "head" of the salt readily mixes with water, but the hydrocarbon-like "body" pushes water away. When soap is mixed with water, the non-polar chains cluster together in a ball or sphere that creates a pocket (called a micelle) where water is excluded, but where non-polar materials are especially attracted. The ionic heads of the individual soap chains cover the surface of the micelle interacting with water molecules. Since food grease, human body oils, and a host of other organic materials are typically present on soiled laundry, the non-polar soap micelles provide a safe harbor for the organic "dirt." At the same time, the polar surface of the micelle attracts it to the wash water, so the entrapped non-polar materials end up being thrown out with the laundry water.

Today, very little soap is actually sold. (Ivory™ Soap is one well-known authentic soap.) Most cleaning agents commonly called soap are actually detergents, which are synthetic materials made from petroleum and sulfuric acid. Look at the ingredient list on a bottle of hand soap, shampoo, or other cleaning product; you probably will see terms such as "sodium lauryl sulfate" or "linear alkylbenzenesulfonates."

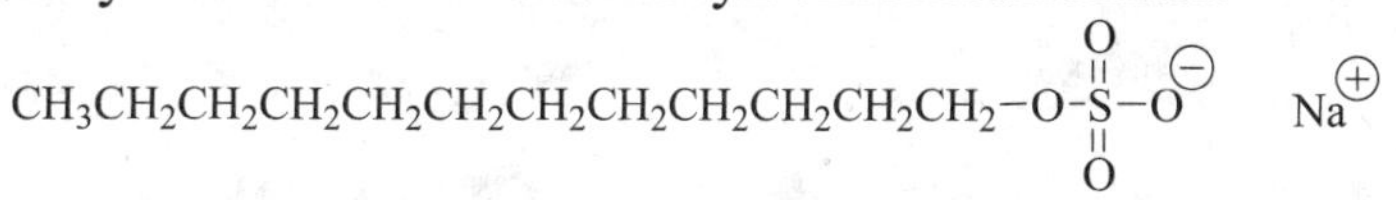

sodium lauryl sulfate

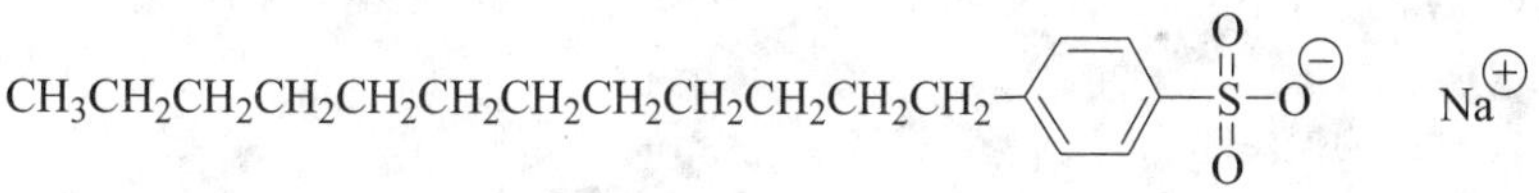

sodium dodecylbenzenesulfonate

These synthetic materials are easier and cheaper to make on a large scale than traditional "soap," and the starting materials are not dependent on a supply of livestock fat! Nonetheless, detergents clean the same way soaps do: They form micelles in water.

Another commercial use for plant-derived triacylglycerides is becoming increasingly more important as global competition for scarcer supplies of petroleum increases—production of *bio-diesel* fuel. When an oil (e.g., soybean, sunflower, or corn) is treated with an excess of an alcohol and an acid as catalyst, *transesterification* occurs, a reaction in which one ester is converted to another. Typically, ethyl alcohol (made from grain or cellulose-containing agricultural waste) or methyl alcohol is used. The reaction equation is shown below.

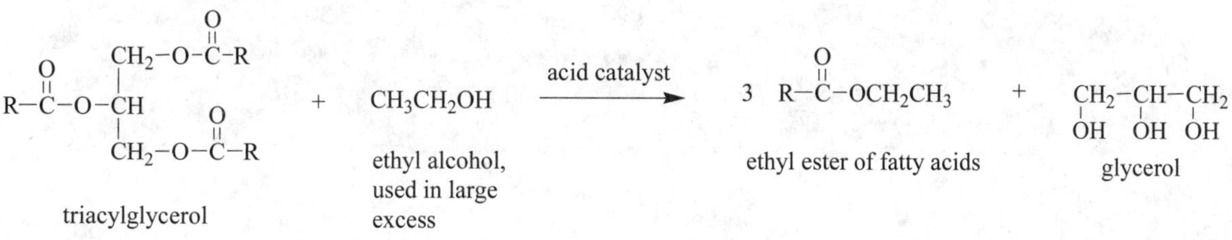

The mixture of ethyl esters of the fatty acids recovered from the reaction is ordinarily blended with petroleum-derived diesel to be sold as bio-diesel, although it can be used as an outright diesel substitute. The great advantage of bio-diesel is that it does not require any modification of the vehicle's diesel engine before it can be burned as fuel. By contrast, automobile engines designed to run on gasoline can not burn ethanol or fuels containing a high proportion of alcohol.

After reading this essay you may think about the words "fat" and "oil" in an entirely new light. The very same substances we associate with food can be used to keep us clean and on the petroleum-free highway to the future.

Background

Lard is the purified fat from the abdomen of a hog. It was traditionally used as the favorite "shortening" for making flaky pie crusts. You may be relieved to know that it is seldom used in commercial food products these days. For home baking, lard has largely been replaced by products containing partially hydrogenated soybean oil (e.g., Crisco™ solid shortening).

Triglycerides are not very soluble in water, so in this experiment the fat will be dissolved in some ethyl alcohol to increase its solubility before it is mixed with the aqueous NaOH. Heating the fat solution with the concentrated base also causes the saponification reaction to take place fairly quickly.

The crude soap formed in the saponification reaction is made less soluble in water by adding a solution of "brine" (a concentrated solution of NaCl in water). Then the precipitated solid is easily collected by filtration, washed clean, and tested.

Working Safely

Do not taste the samples of lard, shortening, or other fats that have been brought into the lab since they may have been contaminated with other chemicals. Place any excess fats in the waste bottle set aside for this purpose.

The alcohol used as a solvent is flammable, so no open flames may be used during this experiment! Wash off alcohol spilled on your skin with cool water. Do not ingest any of the lab alcohol; it is frequently treated with other chemicals to make it poisonous to drink. Follow your instructor's directions for the proper disposal of waste alcohol in your locality.

Sodium hydroxide solution is caustic, which means it can cause a chemical burn if left in contact with the skin. The base used in this experiment is very concentrated, and the hot mixture used to saponify the fat is potentially dangerous if spilled on the skin. Wear disposable gloves if they are available, and keep your fingers out of your ears, nose, eyes, and mouth.

You must wear eye protection at all times when NaOH solution is being used (by you or a nearby worker). If base is splashed in your eyes, immediately flush them at the eyewash fountain for at least 10 minutes. Someone should alert your instructor so that a health care professional can examine your eyes after they have been flushed.

Finally, do not attempt to wash your skin with the soap made in lab since it has not been purified sufficiently to be safe to use.

Procedure

1. Weigh out about 1 g of lard or solid shortening (like Crisco or a similar product) into a 100-mL beaker. (Record the mass of fat used if your instructor asks you to determine the mass of the dry soap later.)

2. Add 2–3 mL of 95% ethanol to the fat. (Use either a 10-mL graduated cylinder or a plastic transfer pipette.)

3. Place the beaker in a bath of hot water on an electric hot plate or steambath. (No open flames!) Stir the mixture with a glass rod until the solid melts and dissolves in the alcohol.

4. Temporarily remove the beaker from the bath. Measure 2 mL of 6 M NaOH with a 10-mL graduated cylinder or plastic transfer pipette, and add the base to the fat solution. [**Warning**: Be especially cautious around the hot base from this step on.]

5. Return the beaker to the hot water bath and stir the mixture constantly with a glass rod until a solid, pasty mass is obtained. Avoid splashing the mixture out of the beaker.

6. Add 12–13 mL of distilled or deionized water to the solid in the beaker. Continue heating and stirring the mixture until a solution is obtained. *If necessary*, you may add no more than 2 mL extra water to dissolve the solids.

7. Remove the beaker from the steambath and place it on the bench. While the mixture is still warm, stir in 10 mL of brine (saturated aqueous NaCl). The soap should precipitate as a solid. Let the mixture cool to room temperature.

8. Assemble the apparatus for collecting a solid by suction (vacuum) filtration as shown in Figure 18-1. Add a piece of filter paper to the funnel and moisten it with water.

9. Apply a vacuum to the filtration apparatus. Cautiously pour the mixture of soap and salt water into the funnel. Remember that the liquid is very basic—continue wearing your eye protection and gloves.

10. Rinse the solid soap in the funnel 4 or 5 times with 5-mL portions of cold water to flush away NaOH trapped in the product. Using a spatula or cork, press down on the solid to squeeze out the last traces of the liquid.

11. Let air back into the filtration apparatus and disconnect the vacuum source. Transfer the solid soap to a piece of filter paper or a watch glass.
-OR-
11. Weigh a clean watch glass and record its mass. Transfer the soap to the watch glass and set it aside to dry until the next lab period. Then determine the mass of soap obtained.

12. Carefully transfer the filtrate (the liquid separated from the solid soap) to a waste container provided by your instructor.

Perform these steps to test your soap:

13. Transfer a spatula-tip of the solid soap to a 15- x 150-mm test tube. Add 5 mL of distilled or deionized water and close the mouth of the tube with a cork or rubber stopper. Shake the solid and water together for several minutes. Record your observations on the Worksheet.

14. Remove a drop of the soap solution on the tip of a clean glass rod from the test tube. Touch the drop to a strip of multi-pH test paper. Record the pH on the Worksheet. For comparison, test the pH of either cold tap water and/or distilled water.

15. Transfer 1–2 mL of the liquid from the large test tube in step 13 to a 12- x 75-mm test tube. Add about 5 drops of 5% $CaCl_2$ (calcium chloride) solution, and gently shake the tube to mix the liquids. Record what you observe on the Worksheet.

16. Transfer 1-2 mL of the liquid from the large test tube in step 13 to another 12- x 75-mm test tube. Now add 5 drops of 5% $MgCl_2$ (magnesium chloride) solution, and gently shake the tube to mix the liquids. Record what you observe on the Worksheet.

17. Your instructor will provide you a dilute solution of sodium lauryl sulfate, a synthetic detergent. Repeat the tests in steps 14, 15, and 16 and record your observations on the Worksheet.

18. Place the leftover solid soap in the container provided by your instructor. Do not dispose of the soap in the trash, sink, or take it from the lab. It is not pure enough to be used for personal hygiene! Dispose of the testing waste from steps 15 and 16 according to your instructor's directions.

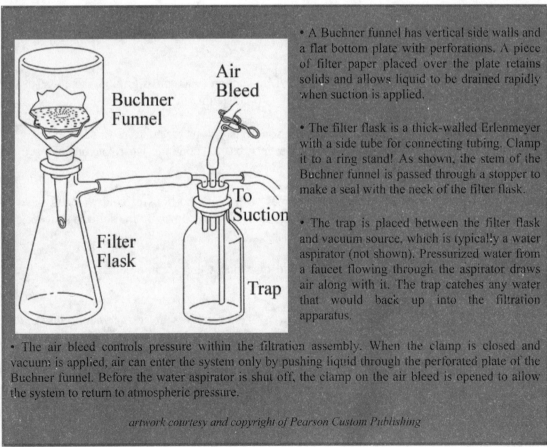

• A Buchner funnel has vertical side walls and a flat bottom plate with perforations. A piece of filter paper placed over the plate retains solids and allows liquid to be drained rapidly when suction is applied.

• The filter flask is a thick-walled Erlenmeyer with a side tube for connecting tubing. Clamp it to a ring stand! As shown, the stem of the Buchner funnel is passed through a stopper to make a seal with the neck of the filter flask.

• The trap is placed between the filter flask and vacuum source, which is typically a water aspirator (not shown). Pressurized water from a faucet flowing through the aspirator draws air along with it. The trap catches any water that would back up into the filtration apparatus.

• The air bleed controls pressure within the filtration assembly. When the clamp is closed and vacuum is applied, air can enter the system only by pushing liquid through the perforated plate of the Buchner funnel. Before the water aspirator is shut off, the clamp on the air bleed is opened to allow the system to return to atmospheric pressure.

artwork courtesy and copyright of Pearson Custom Publishing

Figure 18-1: Apparatus for vacuum filtration

How to Carry out a Vacuum Filtration:

1. Place a piece of filter paper that covers all the perforations in the bottom of the Buchner funnel. Moisten the paper with water if that is the solvent to be separated from the solids.
2. Close the clamp on the air bleed valve. Turn on the water aspirator.
3. Pour the mixture to be filtered into the Buchner funnel. Initially hold the filter paper flat against the funnel bottom with a glass rod to prevent solid from passing through the perforations.
4. When all the liquid has drained from the solid, rinse the solid with some clean solvent.
5. Once liquid no longer drains from the stem of the Buchner funnel, open the valve on the air bleed.
6. After the "whoosh" of air signals that the apparatus has reached room pressure, you can turn off the water aspirator.

Pre-Lab Exercise A
Describe the purpose of the experiment in a few complete sentences of your own phrasing.

Pre-Lab Exercise B
Make a list of the chemicals and equipment you need for this experiment.

Pre-Lab Exercise C
The ester isopentyl acetate (structure at the right) is used as artificial banana flavoring. What are the structures of the alcohol and carboxylic acid used to make this ester?

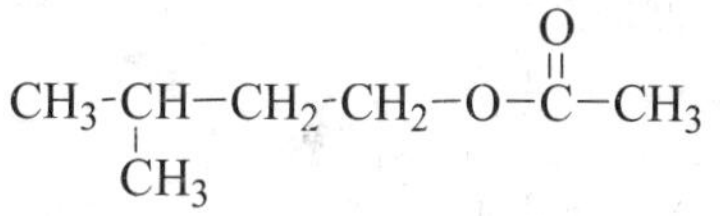

$$CH_3\text{-}CH\text{-}CH_2\text{-}CH_2\text{-}O\text{-}\overset{\overset{\displaystyle O}{\|}}{C}\text{-}CH_3$$
$$\underset{CH_3}{|}$$

Pre-Lab Exercise D
Draw the structure of the triacylglyceride obtained from stearic acid as the only fatty acid.

Pre-Lab Exercise E

Explain how sodium lauryl sulfate can form a micelle in water. Make a simple drawing of a micelle to illustrate your answer.

Pre-Lab Exercise F

How many different fatty acids are obtained by saponification of the triacylglyceride shown here? What are their structures?   Label each fatty acid as saturated or unsaturated.

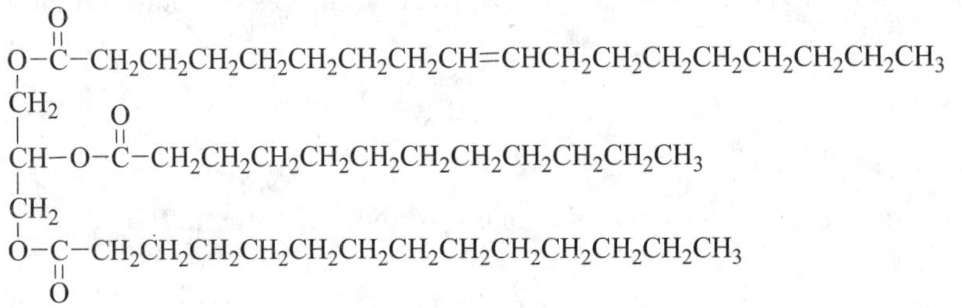

$$O-\overset{\displaystyle O}{\overset{\|}{C}}-CH_2CH_2CH_2CH_2CH_2CH_2CH_2CH=CHCH_2CH_2CH_2CH_2CH_2CH_2CH_2CH_3$$

$$CH_2$$

$$CH-O-\overset{\displaystyle O}{\overset{\|}{C}}-CH_2CH_2CH_2CH_2CH_2CH_2CH_2CH_2CH_2CH_2CH_3$$

$$CH_2$$

$$O-\overset{}{C}-CH_2CH_2CH_2CH_2CH_2CH_2CH_2CH_2CH_2CH_2CH_2CH_2CH_3$$
$$\overset{\|}{O}$$

Pre-Lab Exercise G

Why does adding brine (a saturated aqueous solution of NaCl) to a mixture of soap in water cause the soap to precipitate as a solid?

Pre-Lab Exercise H

Look back to the structure of the triacylglyceride in Exercise F. Draw the structures of the fatty esters obtained when ethyl alcohol is used to convert this fat to bio-diesel.

Lab Worksheet   Name: _____   Section: _____

1. What type of triacylglyceride did you use to make soap?

2. Complete this data table *if* your instructor asks you to determine the mass of the soap after it has dried.

Mass of fat used for making soap	g
Mass of empty watch glass or plate	g
Mass of watch glass and dry soap	g
Net mass of dry soap obtained	g

3. In step 13 of the procedure you mixed some of your soap with water. Did all the soap dissolve? Why is the soap not highly soluble in water?

    Did the soap raise a foam or make bubbles?
    Even if your soap did not make foam or bubbles, suggest why soap promotes longer lived bubbles than form in pure water alone. (It has to do with the properties of soap discussed in this chapter!)

4. Record the results of testing water, soap, and detergent in the table below (procedure steps 14–17). Then use your observations to answer the questions below.

Test	Result for Water	Result for Soap	Result for Detergent
pH			
Addition of 5% $CaCl_2$			
Addition of 5% $MgCl_2$			

    Pioneers on the American frontier who washed their hair with soap made by your procedure often followed up with a rinse of vinegar (acetic acid solution). Why?

    "Hard water" contains significant concentrations of Ca^{2+} and Mg^{2+} ions. If someone uses soap instead of detergent, why is there more soap "scum" to be cleaned off the shower and tub walls?

    Why would clothes washed in hard water with soap need further treatment before the clothes could be dried and worn?

5. *This question is relevant if you weighed and recorded the masses of the fat and the soap in your experiment.*

    A typical "bath size" bar of soap weighs about 125 g. Assuming that the bar is 100% soap, how much fat would be needed to make a bar based on your results in this experiment?

6. If more than one kind or source of fat was used during your lab to make soap, are there any apparent differences in the soap obtained? You could use these criteria for comparison: physical appearance; ease of precipitation and/or filtration of the soap; hardness of the dried soap grains; pH; relative reaction with $CaCl_2$ and $MgCl_2$.

Companion Sections in Waldron: Chapters 11.2, 11.3, 12.1, and 12.4

Introduction

Milk has been called the "perfect food" because it supplies water, protein, carbohydrate, fat, and needed minerals. The composition of milk varies from one species of mammal to another, notably in the relative proportion of protein, fat, and carbohydrate. For example, human milk has a higher percentage of carbohydrate and a lower relative amount of protein than is found in cow's milk. Even so, milk from a cow or goat has a composition more like human milk than most other species.

The vast majority of Americans no longer live on farms and have direct knowledge of the origin of their food, but you probably know that cream (the fat or triacylglycerides) mostly separates from milk. Whole milk purchased in a grocery store has been *homogenized*; that is, the fat particles have been dispersed as tiny droplets in the aqueous milk mixture. On the other hand, skim milk is fat-free.

While milk is a liquid, it most definitely is not a solution. Solutions are clear mixtures having a uniform composition whose constituents can not be separated by simple filtration (Waldron Chapter 1.3). Instead, milk is a colloidal suspension. Colloids are substances of high molecular mass that do not dissolve in a solvent completely to make a clear mixture. Colloid particles are small enough that they do not settle from the mixture as would clumps of dirt mixed with water. A beam of light passed into a colloidal suspension will be scattered, while the same beam passes through a true solution.

The colloids in milk are principally the proteins casein and albumin. Recall that proteins are long chain polymers made from amino acids linked together by formation of amides between the carboxyl group of one acid and the amino group of a second amino acid (Waldron Chapters 10.4 and 10.5). The example below shows the formation of a pentapeptide from 5 amino acids.

Five different amino acids, where R represents the structure of the groups found in the 20 basic amino acids

$$H_2N-\underset{R^1}{\overset{\overset{\displaystyle O}{\|}}{CH-C}}-OH \qquad H_2N-\underset{R^2}{\overset{\overset{\displaystyle O}{\|}}{CH-C}}-OH \qquad H_2N-\underset{R^3}{\overset{\overset{\displaystyle O}{\|}}{CH-C}}-OH \qquad H_2N-\underset{R^4}{\overset{\overset{\displaystyle O}{\|}}{CH-C}}-OH \qquad H_2N-\underset{R^5}{\overset{\overset{\displaystyle O}{\|}}{CH-C}}-OH$$

An enzyme catalyzes formation of amide bonds with loss of water.

- H_2O

$$H_2N-\underset{R^1}{\overset{\overset{\displaystyle O}{\|}}{CH-C}}-NH-\underset{R^2}{\overset{\overset{\displaystyle O}{\|}}{CH-C}}-NH-\underset{R^3}{\overset{\overset{\displaystyle O}{\|}}{CH-C}}-NH-\underset{R^4}{\overset{\overset{\displaystyle O}{\|}}{CH-C}}-NH-\underset{R^5}{\overset{\overset{\displaystyle O}{\|}}{CH-C}}-OH \qquad + \; 5\,H_2O$$

A pentapeptide

Casein and albumin are much larger than the simple pentapeptide shown above. If all the side chain groups in the example were CH_3, the molecular mass of the pentapeptide would be 373. In comparison, the molecular mass of casein is about 26,000 and the value for albumin is about twice as large!

The very long chains of peptides and proteins twist and fold upon themselves into compact forms under the influence of intermolecular forces such as hydrogen bonds (Waldron Chapter 7.2). The folding and twisting of protein chains typically results in a shape that makes the polymer more soluble in water because the groups on the outer surface of the protein are those most able to interact with water by making hydrogen bonds. When the solution containing a soluble protein is heated or mixed with acid, base, or ionic compounds, the protein is often *denatured* (caused to unfold from its natural shape), and it becomes insoluble as a consequence. Milk "sours" because bacteria have produced lactic acid, and curds of protein begin to separate from the liquid as the change in acidity causes some denaturation.

The major carbohydrate in milk is called lactose ("milk sugar"). Lactose itself is formed by the enzymatic union of two simpler sugars, glucose and galactose. As illustrated below, glucose and galactose exist as six-atom ring monosaccharides. An enzyme in the mammary gland connects the β-anomer of galactose specifically and exclusively to the oxygen atom on carbon 4 of the glucose ring. Lactose is shown in the form in which it is obtained when it crystallizes from solution.

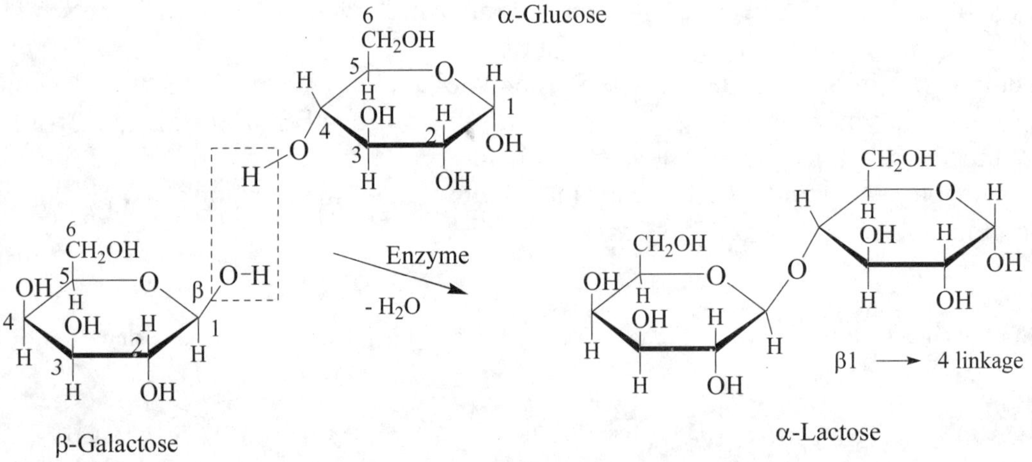

Interestingly, the arrangement of OH groups around the ring of galactose and glucose differs at position-4 on the ring. (Both sugars have α and β anomers present in solution.) People of northern European descent usually have an enzyme that converts galactose into glucose before it can be metabolized; those who lack this enzyme are lactose-intolerant and must restrict their intake of dairy products or take an enzyme supplement.

Very likely you have seen advertisements on television or in print which extol dairy products as a good source of calcium, which is needed for the growth and maintenance of bone and teeth. Calcium ions are found in milk in two forms: as free ions of Ca^{2+} in solution and as calcium ions tightly associated with proteins like casein (called "bound Ca^{2+}"). Magnesium ions are also present in a lower concentration in milk, since numerous enzymes use Mg^{2+} as a cofactor or assistant for their function.

Background

In this experiment you will denature and precipitate casein by warming skim (fat-free) milk with some dilute acetic acid. The protein can be collected by filtration, dried, and weighed to estimate its percentage contribution to liquid milk.

The acid-induced precipitation of protein from milk is similar to the process used for making cheese; the liquid remaining after this step, traditionally called *whey*, contains carbohydrates, minerals, and other water-soluble components of milk. Although it is possible to recover the α-lactose from the whey, the process is involved and time-consuming. However, it is not necessary to physically isolate the carbohydrate component of milk to demonstrate its presence.

In the 19th century scientists discovered that useful information about carbohydrates could be obtained by observing their reaction with solutions containing Cu^{2+}. Copper, like other transition metals, forms more than one kind of ion. Copper(II) or Cu^{2+} is the more common ion, and its aqueous solutions have a characteristic blue color. The less common ion is Cu^{+}.

Now, here is where things get interesting. When a clear blue solution of Cu^{2+} is heated with some types of carbohydrates, the Cu^{2+} is converted to Cu^{+} that precipitates from solution as the reddish-brown oxide, Cu_2O. The reaction $Cu^{2+} \rightarrow Cu^{+}$ is classified as a *reduction* since each Cu^{2+} gains one electron to lower (reduce) its charge to Cu^{+} (Waldron Chapter 2.5).

The electrons needed to reduce Cu^{2+} must come from another substance. Thus, a carbohydrate that is able to reduce Cu^{2+} to Cu_2O is called a *reducing sugar*. "What becomes of the carbohydrate?" The sugar which loses or gives up electrons is oxidized and forms a carbohydrate containing a C=O. (The exact structure of this substance is not relevant to our experiment.)

More important, not all carbohydrates are reducing sugars. Only sugars which have an OH group at the anomeric carbon (the one next to the oxygen in the ring) are capable of being oxidized, so only these sugars can reduce Cu^{2+} to Cu_2O. A combination of $CuSO_4$, citric acid, and sodium hydroxide called *Benedict's Reagent* is commonly used to test for the presence of a reducing sugar. This reagent is particularly useful since few other materials besides carbohydrates will cause a reddish precipitate of Cu_2O to form. In this experiment you will compare the reaction behavior of whey, a known sample of lactose, and several other sugars (glucose, fructose, and sucrose) with Benedict's reagent.

Finally, we noted earlier that milk contains Ca^{2+} and some Mg^{2+}. A qualitative test can verify the presence of these ions in the whey without actually having to separate them from the other components. Reactions that produce color changes or precipitates are most often employed for qualitative tests.

The dye *calmagite* is an acid-base indicator having a blue color in solution at pH 10. (Refer back to the discussion in Experiment 10.) If Ca^{2+} or Mg^{2+} is also present, the attraction between the oppositely charged indicator and metal ions is strong enough to alter how electrons are delocalized in the dye, and the color changes as a result.

Calmagite   Calmagite in solution at pH 10; Blue color   Calmagite at pH 10 associated with Ca^{2+} or Mg^{2+}; Pink-red color

These observations suggest a simple qualitative test to determine if Ca^{2+} and/or Mg^{2+} are in a solution. The sample to be tested is adjusted to pH 10 by the addition of some ammonia solution (NH_3 and NH_4Cl in water). Then a few drops of calmagite indicator are added: If the solution stays blue, there is no Mg^{2+} or Ca^{2+} present; a pink-red color means at least one of these ions is present. Since the perception of color can vary from person to person and under different circumstances, it is good laboratory practice to perform comparison tests with solutions known to contain the materials being tested. And so, you will compare the calmagite test on whey with solutions known to contain Mg^{2+} and Ca^{2+} and with ion-free water as a "blank" or "control."

Working Safely

Although milk and milk proteins are normally safe to eat, do not consume any of the milk or casein used in this lab since they may have been contaminated.

Wear proper eye protection during the lab (safety glasses or goggles), and note the location of the nearest eye wash fountain. Keep your fingers out of your eyes, ears, nose, and mouth during lab.

The acetic acid solution used in the experiment is just slightly more concentrated than ordinary table vinegar, though its odor may be more noticeable. If you spill any of this weak acid on your skin, flush it off with cold water for several minutes. No permanent harm should result.

Benedict's solution contains Cu^{2+} and is alkaline (basic). Avoid skin contact with the solution, and wash any spills off with water right away. If the mixture is splashed in your eyes, rinse them for 5–10 minutes at the eye wash fountain; then consult your instructor about being examined by a health care provider.

The pH 10 ammonia solution is also basic: Avoid contact with skin and eyes. The ammonia fumes may also be irritating to your nose and eyes, so please keep the bottle capped when you are not dispensing the solution.

Calmagite can stain your skin; wearing gloves is recommended when you use this indicator dye.

Procedure

Separation of Casein from Skim Milk

1. Weigh a 150-mL beaker and record its mass in the Data Table 1 on the Worksheet.

2. Measure out 25 mL of skim milk in a graduated cylinder, and transfer it to the 150-mL beaker.

3. Determine the mass of the beaker and the contained milk on the same balance used to weigh the empty beaker. Record the total mass in Data Table 1.

4. Add approximately 5 mL of 1 M acetic acid solution to the milk in the beaker. The volume can be measured with a 10-mL graduated cylinder or even a plastic transfer pipette. Excess or waste acetic acid solution can be neutralized with baking soda ($NaHCO_3$, sodium bicarbonate) and flushed down the sink unless local laws prohibit this method of disposal.

5. Set the beaker of acidified milk in a pan, tub, or 250-mL beaker partially filled with warm water (40–50° C; from hot water faucet is fine). Stir the mixture with a plastic spoon or glass rod for about 5 minutes until the protein begins to separate from the yellow liquid whey.

6. Cut or tear a crude 12-cm diameter circle from a white or unbleached paper towel like those used in the kitchen or a rest room, and fold it into a filter cone to fit inside a short-stemmed funnel. This type of paper has the large, coarse pores needed to filter the protein from the whey rapidly. (Regular laboratory grade filter paper will become plugged.)

7. Support the funnel over a 125-mL Erlenmeyer flask, and then pour the precipitated protein and the whey into the paper-lined funnel. Scrape out the protein clinging to the walls of the beaker and add it to the mixture in the funnel.

8. Once the liquid has drained from the protein, label the Erlenmeyer flask of whey and set it aside. Place another container under the funnel stem before rinsing the protein with about 25 mL of distilled water. The rinse water may be discarded in the sink.

9. Lift the paper covered by protein from the funnel and set it aside on several thicknesses of paper towel to dry, ideally overnight.

10. Weigh a watch glass or plastic weighing boat and record its mass in Data Table 1.

11. Carefully peel the dried protein away from the paper and collect it in the container in step 10. Determine the mass of the container and protein, and record the weight in Data Table 1.

12. Place the casein in the trash can (if allowed) or a waste container provided by your instructor.

Benedict's Test for Carbohydrates
13. Obtain five 15- x 150-mm test tubes and label them W, L, G, S, and F, respectively.

14. Using a clean glass or plastic transfer pipette each time, add:
    1 mL of Whey from your 125-mL Erlenmeyer in step 8 to tube W;
    1 mL of aqueous 1% Lactose solution to tube L;
    1 mL of aqueous 1% Glucose solution to tube G;
    1 mL of aqueous 1% Sucrose solution to tube S; and
    1 mL of aqueous 1% Fructose solution to tube F.
    (Excess portions of any of these solutions may be flushed down the sink.)

15. Add 5 mL of the prepared Benedict's reagent to each of the test tubes in step 14, and gently shake the tubes to mix the liquids.

16. As soon as tubes W, L, G, S, and F have been prepared in step 15, place them together at the same time in a 400- or 600-mL beaker of water (hot or cold). Bring the water to boil in the beaker over moderately high heat. Note the time you started heating the tubes near Data Table 2 on the Worksheet.

17. When you notice the formation of a reddish-brown precipitate in a test tube, note the time in Data Table 2. Pay no attention to the color of the liquid. Using a test tube holder, remove the tube from the hot water bath and set it on a rack to cool.

18. Do not assume that all the tubes should contain a precipitate. Stop heating after 10–12 minutes whether or not any precipitate has formed.

19. Pour the contents of tubes W, L, G, S, and F into the container marked "Benedict's Test Waste."

Protein, Carbohydrate, and Minerals in Milk

Testing for Magnesium and Calcium Ions

20. Label each of four 13- x 100-mm test tubes as H_2O, Mg, Ca, and W, respectively.

21. Add: 2 mL of deionized or distilled water to the tube H_2O ;
    2 mL of 1% aqueous $MgCl_2$ solution to the tube Mg ;
    2 mL of 1% aqueous $CaCl_2$ solution to the tube Ca ; and
    2 mL of whey solution (from step 8) to tube W.

22. From a small dispensing bottle with a dropper tip, add 5–10 drops of pH 10 solution (NH_3 and NH_4Cl in water) to each tube in step 21.

23. Finally add 4–5 drops of calmagite indicator to each tube in step 22.

24. Gently agitate or shake each of the test tubes until the solution has a uniform color. Record the observed color of each solution in Data Table 3.

25. The solutions in tubes H_2O, Mg, Ca, and W may be flushed down the sink unless local regulations require them to be placed in a separate waste container.

Pre-Lab Exercise A

Describe the purpose of the experiment in a few complete sentences of your own phrasing.

Pre-Lab Exercise B

Make a list of the chemicals and equipment needed for this experiment.

Pre-Lab Exercise C

Explain why adding acid or base to a protein solution may cause the protein to precipitate.

Pre-Lab Exercise D

What types of atom groups must be present in a compound in order for it to form hydrogen bonds? Why are proteins particularly capable of making hydrogen bonds?

Pre-Lab Exercise E

Examine the structures of the carbohydrates below.
(1) Label each sugar as a monosaccharide or disaccharide.
(2) Mark each anomeric carbon with a *.
(3) Explain why each carbohydrate is expected to be a "reducing sugar."

Pre-Lab Exercise F

A copy of the structure of calmagite indicator at pH 10 is given below. The SO_3^- group makes the dye soluble in water, but it is not involved in making the compound colored. Draw a circle around the atoms that are part of the conjugated system.

Pre-Lab Exercise G

Magnesium and calcium compounds are often found together in nature. Suggest a reason why this might be so. **Hint**: Check out your handy Periodic Table. Why do both metals form ions with a +2 charge?

Pre-Lab Exercise H

Two different dipeptides could be formed from the amino acids shown below. Draw the structures of these two dipeptides.

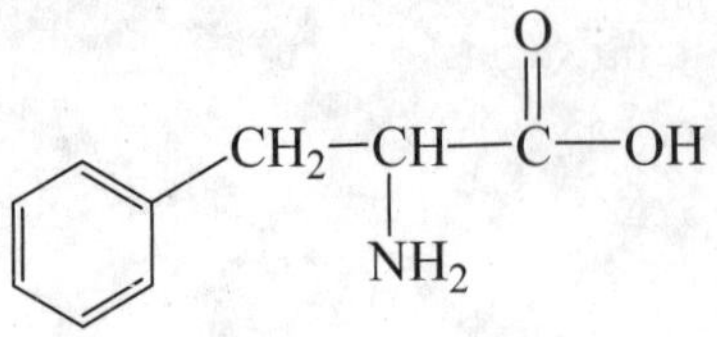

$$CH_2-CH-\overset{\overset{\textstyle O}{\|}}{C}-OH \qquad \text{and} \qquad CH_3-CH-\overset{\overset{\textstyle O}{\|}}{C}-OH$$

(with NH_2 groups below the CH carbons)

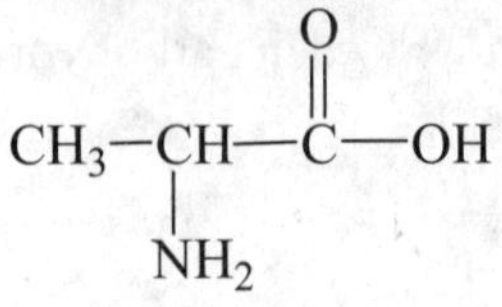

Pre-Lab Exercise I

Imagine that you have 5 molecules of a single monosaccharide and 5 molecules of a single amino acid. Explain why there is only one possible pentapeptide that could be constructed in contrast to the very large number of different pentasaccharides that could be formed.

Pre-Lab Exercise J

Explain why most simple carbohydrates are quite soluble in water but insoluble in liquids such as hexane, and only slightly soluble in ethyl alcohol. **Hint:** Think about intermolecular attractions.

Lab Worksheet   **Name:** _____   **Section:** _____

1. Complete Data Table 1 using the information collected in steps 1–11 of the Procedure.

   Data Table 1: Separation of casein from milk

Mass of empty 150-mL beaker =		g
Mass of beaker + 25 mL skim milk =		g
Mass of milk used =		g
Mass of empty container for casein =		g
Mass of container + dry casein =		g
Mass of casein obtained from milk =		g

2. What is the percentage by weight of casein in milk based on the data in Table 1?
   Recall that a weight percentage describes how many grams of a substance are found in 100 grams of a mixture. Show your work.

3. Cow's milk has about 3 to 3.5% protein by weight. How well does your finding compare with this information?

   Offer an explanation why your answer would probably be too large if the weight of the casein was determined immediately after the protein was precipitated from the milk.

4. Record the observations from Benedict's test in Data Table 2 below.

   Starting time for heating tubes in water bath = _____ (hour:minutes)

   Data Table 2: Results of Benedict's test

Tube	Sugar Tested	Time Tube Removed from Bath (hour:min)	Red-Brown Precipitate Seen? Y or N
W			
L			
G			
S			
F			

5. Which of the carbohydrates tested were reducing sugars?

   Which of the carbohydrates were non-reducing sugars?

6. Did the lactose and whey samples react the same in Benedict's test?

    If whey is known from other research to contain lactose, why might the reaction behavior of whey and pure lactose solution in Benedict's test not be identical?

7. The structures of glucose and lactose were given earlier. Are your results for these sugars in Data Table 2 consistent with the structures of the carbohydrates? Explain why or why not.

8. Fructose (structure below) contains 6 carbon atoms, but is commonly found as a 5-atom ring sugar.

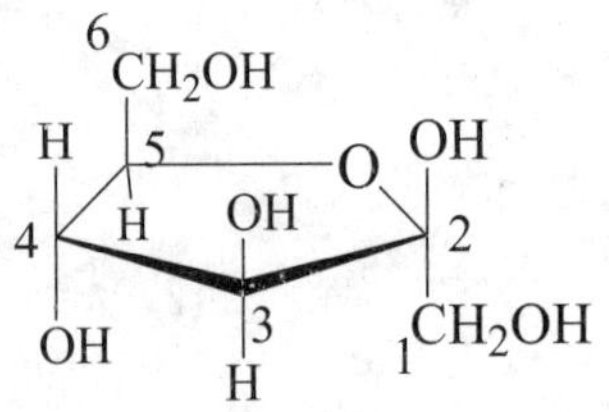

    Put a * next to the anomeric carbon in the fructose structure.
    Is fructose a monosaccharide or disaccharide?

    Are your results from Benedict's test consistent with the structure? Explain.

9. What is suggested by the result of Benedict's test on sucrose (ordinary table sugar)?

    Sucrose (structure below) is a disaccharide formed from glucose and fructose. Identify which ring in the sketch represents each sugar.
    Place an * next to any anomeric carbon in the structure.

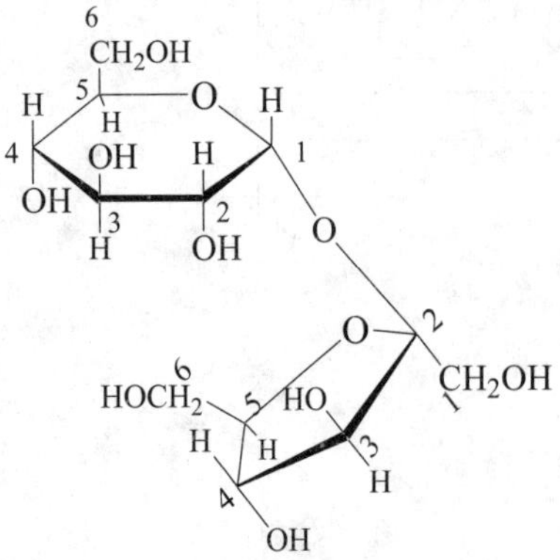

    Are the results of your Benedict's test on sucrose consistent with this structure?

    Explain.

10. Record your observations from testing with calmagite (steps 20–24) in Data Table 3 below.

Data Table 3: Indicator tests for Ca^{2+} and Mg^{2+}

Tube	Color Seen for Calmagite Indicator at pH 10
H_2O	
Mg	
Ca	
W	

What is the color of the indicator in basic solution in the absence of calcium or magnesium ions?

Do Ca^{2+} and Mg^{2+} cause the same color change for the indicator?

Can this test differentiate between magnesium and calcium?

Explain why you can not tell if milk contains more calcium than magnesium based on these results.

Introduction

Pain is one of the oldest enemies of humankind, and even today it is not always an easy foe to fight since there are multiple causes and types of pain. A significant number of people suffer from pains that appear to have no medical explanation. Throughout history humans have used both physical and chemical techniques to manage or dull pain: massage, hot and cold packs, acupuncture, meditation, alcoholic beverages, opium, and cocaine, among others. The variety of techniques for dealing with pain reflects the varied sources and types of pains we can experience, the relative ineffectiveness of any one method of relief for all types of pain, and the undesired side-effects of the treatment.

Fever, headache, and muscle soreness are among some of the most common pains we endure. Sometime in the past people discovered that drinking a tea made from the bark of the willow tree was helpful in dealing with the aches and pains that accompanied winter ailments like colds and flu. Unfortunately, the brew is bitter and harsh on the stomach. Research by German chemists in the late nineteenth century elucidated the structure of the active ingredient in willow bark tea. Once the structure was known, the chemists of the time investigated ways to chemically modify the substance to create a less irritating, but still effective, pain reducer. The result was acetylsalicylic acid, or what we more commonly call *aspirin*. As you know, aspirin remains a widely used and versatile medicine.

Although aspirin is much less bitter than the willow bark tea it still is a stomach irritant and a "blood thinner" (reduces coagulation). For some people, these side effects rule out aspirin therapy for headache, joint, and fever pain management.

acetylsalisylic acid
"aspirin"

The financial success of aspirin in the marketplace, the increase in medical and chemical knowledge, and the need for alternate pain relievers motivated scientists to seek out other compounds that might complement or replace aspirin. While that search continues unabated even today, there are now several other compounds routinely available for treating mild pain, such as acetaminophen, ibuprofen, and naproxen.

acetaminophen   ibuprofen   naproxen

These are the active ingredients in the common products Tylenol® (acetaminophen), Advil® (ibuprofen), and Alleve® (naproxen).

Background

The balanced equation for the reaction used to prepare acetaminophen is shown below.

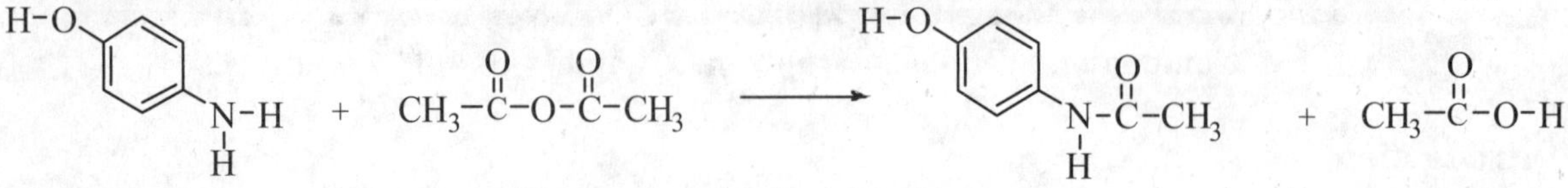

| *para*-aminophenol | acetic anhydride | | acetaminophen | acetic acid |

"Balanced" means that the same number and kinds of atoms appear to the left and to the right of the equation arrow. Chemical reactions are governed by the law of conservation of mass. Thus, chemical reactions do not destroy and create atoms, but rearrange them to form new substances from existing ones. This equation also tells us that one molecule of *para*-aminophenol and one molecule of acetic anhydride react to produce one molecule of acetaminophen and one molecule of acetic acid. If we wish to make acetaminophen, the acetic acid is a "by-product" that must be removed to obtain a pure product.

The *para*-aminophenol contains two functional groups, the phenol (the –OH end of the molecule) and the amine (the –NH_2). The amine group is much more reactive towards the C=O group of the acetic anhydride; as a result one acetyl group (the CH_3C=O) is transferred to the nitrogen atom, while the other acetyl group and a hydrogen from nitrogen leave to make acetic acid. When this reaction takes place in water, the acetaminophen precipitates or crystallizes from solution because it is not very soluble. The acetic acid is very soluble in water and remains dissolved. Hence, the two products are easily separated by filtering the mixture when the reaction is completed.

Working Safely

Wear safety glasses or goggles while performing the experiment. Using disposable gloves is recommended since the chemicals needed are irritants on contact with the skin. Avoid putting your fingers in your mouth, eyes, ears, or nose during this lab. The vapors of acetic anhydride can act like tear gas on the eyes. At the conclusion of the lab follow your instructor's directions for disposal of the waste liquid from the filtration. The acetaminophen you make will not be pharmaceutically pure, nor of an appropriate dose for human use: Do not take it from lab or ingest it! Place your product in the container the instructor provides when you have finished the lab.

Procedure

1. Weigh 0.33–0.35 g *para*-aminophenol onto a piece of paper or into a plastic weighing boat. Record the actual mass of the solid used in the Data Table on the Worksheet.

2. Transfer all the solid into a 16- x 150-mm test tube.

3. Obtain 1–2 mL of 7% aqueous acetic acid with a plastic transfer pipette or a 10-mL graduated cylinder. Add all of the dilute acetic acid to the solid in the test tube.

4. Gently agitate the tube to mix the liquid and solid, but do not expect the solid to dissolve.

Reminders:

Wear gloves to avoid skin contact with the solid. Keep the gloves on from this point.

—

Any volume in this range is acceptable. The dilute acid is being used as the reaction solvent, not as a reactant.

—

5. Working in a hood or a well-ventilated area, measure out 0.5 mL of acetic anhydride using another *dry* pipette. Add this to the tube containing the *para*-aminophenol and aqueous acetic acid. Gently agitate the tube to mix the contents.

> Your instructor may provide the acetic anhydride in a smaller dropper bottle instead. Use 10 drops = 0.5 mL.
>
> ───

6. Clamp the test tube in a 250-mL beaker half-filled with water. Heat the water on a hot plate to 70–80° C. (Point the mouth of the test tube away from anyone's face.) Occasionally swirl the tube to mix the contents during the heating.

> *Or*: Fill the beaker with hot or boiling water if it is available. Clamp the tube immersed in the hot water without further heating for 5–7 minutes.

7. Remove the tube from the hot water bath, and let it cool to near room temperature before immersing it in an ice bath.

> ───
>
> Don't let your tube tip over in the ice bath!

8. Set up the apparatus for a vacuum filtration as described in Figure 20-1.

> ───

9. Once the test tube is ice-cold to the touch, it should contain both solid and liquid. If no solid is visible, insert a glass stirring rod into the tube beneath the surface of the liquid. Gently push the glass rod up and down against the wall of the tube. Solid should begin to form right away.

> ───
>
> The solid product is acetaminophen.

10. Place a piece of clean filter paper in the bottom of the filtration funnel, moisten it with some distilled water, and apply suction to the flask. Pour the contents of your test tube into the funnel. Chase the rest of the solid in the test tube into the funnel with a stream of water squirted from a wash bottle.

> ───
>
> The water also helps rinse the remaining solution off of the solid.
>
> ───

11. Admit air into the filter flask before turning off the suction. The filtrate (liquid in the flask) contains water, acetic acid, and some left-over reactants. Place the solution in the proper waste container.

12. Transfer the powdery acetaminophen to a piece of filter paper to dry. When the moisture has been absorbed by the paper, weigh the solid on another dry piece of paper and record the mass of the solid you obtained.

> ───
>
> Do not include the mass of the paper in the weight of the product.

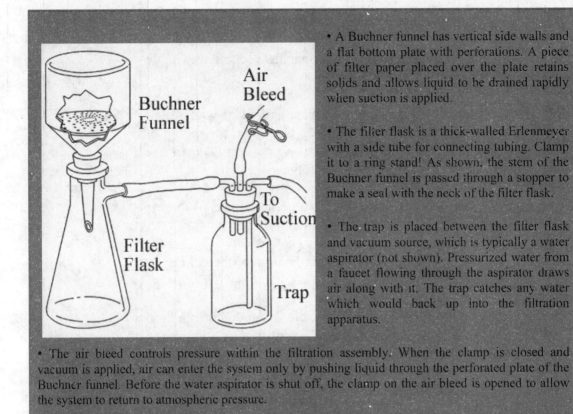

• A Buchner funnel has vertical side walls and a flat bottom plate with perforations. A piece of filter paper placed over the plate retains solids and allows liquid to be drained rapidly when suction is applied.

• The filter flask is a thick-walled Erlenmeyer with a side tube for connecting tubing. Clamp it to a ring stand! As shown, the stem of the Buchner funnel is passed through a stopper to make a seal with the neck of the filter flask.

• The trap is placed between the filter flask and vacuum source, which is typically a water aspirator (not shown). Pressurized water from a faucet flowing through the aspirator draws air along with it. The trap catches any water which would back up into the filtration apparatus.

• The air bleed controls pressure within the filtration assembly. When the clamp is closed and vacuum is applied, air can enter the system only by pushing liquid through the perforated plate of the Buchner funnel. Before the water aspirator is shut off, the clamp on the air bleed is opened to allow the system to return to atmospheric pressure.

artwork courtesy and copyright of Pearson Custom Publishing

Figure 20-1: Apparatus for vacuum filtration

How to Carry out a Vacuum Filtration:

1. Place a piece of filter paper that covers all the perforations in the bottom of the Buchner funnel. Moisten the paper with water if that is the solvent to be filtered.
2. Close the clamp on the air bleed valve. Turn on the water aspirator.
3. Pour the mixture to be filtered into the Buchner funnel. Initially hold the filter paper flat against the funnel bottom with a glass rod to prevent solid from passing through the perforations.
4. When all the liquid has drained from the solid, rinse the solid with some clean solvent.
5. Once liquid no longer drains from the stem of the Buchner funnel, open the valve on the air bleed.
6. After the "whoosh" of air signals that the apparatus has reached room pressure, you can turn off the water aspirator.

Pre-Lab Exercise A

Describe the purpose of the experiment in a few complete sentences of your own phrasing.

Pre-Lab Exercise B
Make a list of the chemicals and equipment needed for this experiment.

Pre-Lab Exercise C
Phenacetin is a pain-relieving compound related to acetaminophen, although it is no longer sold because of safety concerns.

Calculate the molar mass of phenacetin (i.e., its molecular weight) using these atomic weights:

H = 1; C = 12; N =14; and O = 16.

Hint: Review Waldron Chapter 2.4.

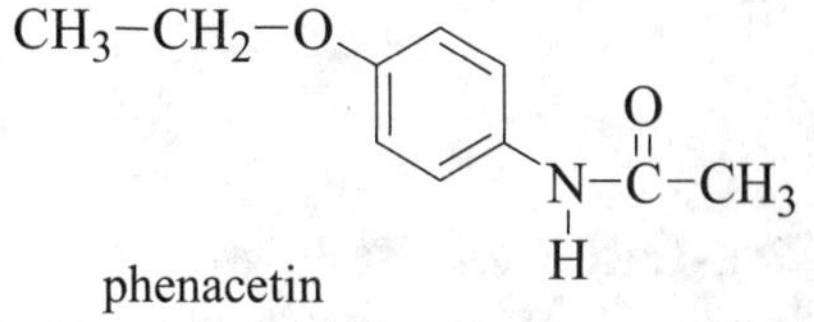

phenacetin

Pre-Lab Exercise D
Phenacetin is prepared from the compound *para*-ethoxyaniline. Calculate the molecular weight of *para*-ethoxyaniline from the same atomic weights given in Pre-Lab Exercise C.

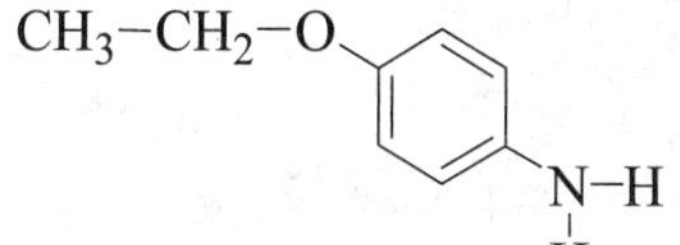

para-ethoxyaniline

Suppose that you were going to make phenacetin starting with 1.00 g of *para*-ethoxyaniline. How many moles of this compound would be used? Show your work below. **Hint**: Review Waldron Chapter 2.4.

Synthesis of Acetaminophen

Pre-Lab Exercise E

The reaction for making phenacetin from *para*-ethoxyaniline is shown here.

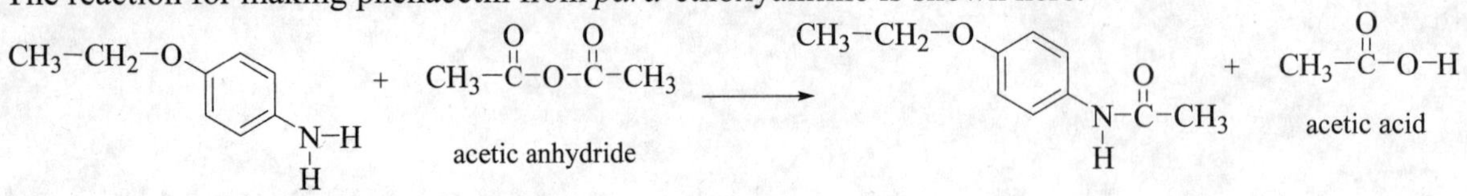

Is this reaction equation balanced? Why or why not? If not, what should the coefficients (multipliers) be in the reaction equation? **Hint**: Review Waldron Chapter 1.2.

Pre-Lab Exercise F

Imagine that you were going to convert 1.00 g of *para*-ethoxyaniline to phenacetin. According to your calculation in Pre-Lab Exercise D and the balanced equation in Pre-Lab Exercise E, what is the minimum number of moles of acetic anhydride needed to react with all the *para*-ethoxyaniline? **Hint**: Review Waldron Chapter 1.2.

Pre-Lab Exercise G

Acetic anhydride has a molecular weight of 102. Based on your answer to Pre-Lab Exercise F, how many grams of acetic anhydride would be needed to react with 1.00 g of *para*-ethoxyaniline? **Hint**: Review Waldron Chapter 2.4.

Acetic anhydride is a liquid having a density of 1.08 g/mL. How many milliliters of acetic anhydride provide the mass you just calculated?

Lab Worksheet   **Name:** _____   **Section:** _____

1. Record the following data in the space provided.

   Mass of *para*-aminophenol used = _____   (Write down as many digits as can be read on the
                                                  balance.)

   Drops or mL of acetic anhydride used = _____   drops or mL (circle one)

   Mass of acetaminophen obtained as product after allowing it to dry = _____

2. Calculate the following and show work in the space provided.

   Molecular weight of *para*-aminophenol = _____
   (See structure given earlier; use rounded whole number atomic weights.)

   Molecular weight of acetic anhydride = _____

   Molecular weight of acetaminophen = _____

   Number of moles *para*-aminophenol used = _____

   Number of grams and moles of acetic anhydride contained in 0.5 mL or 10 drops = _____

   Number of moles of acetaminophen obtained as product = _____

3. Chemists measure how successfully a reaction produces the desired material by calculating the
   percentage yield. This is defined as
   (moles of product actually obtained /maximum possible moles of product) x 100%.

   Explain why the maximum possible moles of acetaminophen you can obtain in this experiment
   equals the moles of *para*-acetaminophen you used.

   Calculate your percentage yield of acetaminophen, showing the work.

4. What functional groups are present in a molecule of acetaminophen?

Why is acetaminophen considered an "aromatic" compound?

Why is the ring in acetaminophen flat and rigid? **Hint**: Review the Models Exercise in Experiment 8 and Waldron Chapter 3.